THEOLOGY AND THE ARTS

Theology and the Arts

By
DAVID BAILY HARNED

THE WESTMINSTER PRESS
Philadelphia

Scripture quotations are from the Revised Standard Version of the Bible, copyright, 1946 and 1952, by the Division of Christian Education of the National Council of Churches, and are used by permission.

Acknowledgment is made to The Macmillan Company for:
The lines quoted from "For Anne Gregory" reprinted from the *Collected Poems of W. B. Yeats;* copyright 1933, The Macmillan Company; renewed 1961 by Bertha Georgie Yeats.
The lines from "A Prayer for Old Age," reprinted from the *Collected Poems of W. B. Yeats;* copyright 1934, The Macmillan Company; renewed 1962 by Bertha Georgie Yeats.
The excerpt from Arthur Koestler, *Darkness at Noon,* tr. by Daphne Hardy; copyright 1941.

LIBRARY OF CONGRESS CATALOG CARD No. 66-15963

Published by The Westminster Press ®
Philadelphia, Pennsylvania

PRINTED IN THE UNITED STATES OF AMERICA

For Elaine

For Elaine

CONTENTS

CONTENTS

PREFACE

This is a report on recent Christian concern with the arts. Although its antecedents lie in romanticism, there is no real precedent for it in the history of the church. It is shaped by pressures and challenges distinctive of our age.

Most Protestant theologians involved in this enterprise have been occupied with the "message" of contemporary literature and painting. They have tended to interpret the artist's venture as a kind of forecourt to religious illumination. Whatever the validity of this approach, it has obscured more urgent reasons for concern with what the artist does. His work sustains our life together. Without him, human society would not survive. *What* he says must be left to his own determination; no one can legislate how the man of letters must view the world. *That* he speaks, not what his message is, should be the principal concern of the Christian community. If we are responsible for the welfare of man in this world, as well as for his destiny in the next, it is important to redress the balance.

I suspect a theological deficiency in the present shape of Protestant concern with the arts. The religious man is always tempted to manipulate reality until he can find some kernel of spiritual significance beneath the husk of things. He is tempted to love the finite more for the impetus it affords his leap toward the infinite than for its own intrinsic importance. He believes he must do more than simply face the particular and circumscribed realities of experience and take them for what they are worth. The artist's venture is a kind of cure for such precipitate spirituality. It makes us rub up against the stubborn but ingratiating whatness of things.

In order to clarify the fundamental options for a Christian interpretation of art and the wider human enterprise, I have dealt with Roman Catholic and Eastern Orthodox as well as Protestant theologians. Each perspective contributes something that no other recognizes so well. But my essential concerns are with the way the man of letters serves our common welfare, and with some problems that beset Protestant theologians when they write of the world that God has made and of the venture in it that he has called man to pursue.

This essay is intended for those who want an aid to reflection about the importance of the arts, and for those who want to know why theologians are concerned with literature and painting and how that concern has been expressed. But it is also written for those more directly involved in the discipline of theology. I am arguing for the recovery of an old article of faith too much ignored by contemporary Protestantism — belief in God as Creator, which ought to constrain men to cherish all the common and ordinary things the Author of nature wills and sustains, and whatever makes this world more fully man's home.

All of us have many teachers. Some of the best are always our students, and I am indebted to mine at Williams, Yale, and Smith. A number of friends have given this essay a reading in one or another of its versions — particularly Professors Julian Hartt and Hans Frei at Yale, Professor Claude Welch at the University of Pennsylvania, and the Rev. Charles G. Titsworth III of Deerfield, Mass.

Most of all, my wife and boys are the ones to thank. Christopher and Timothy provide the reasons to write and to do all other things, and have cheerfully survived the way I neglected them while in the midst of this.

D. B. H.

Northampton, Massachusetts

I

THEOLOGY AND THE
MAN OF LETTERS

THE BEGINNINGS OF A NEW ADVENTURE

Every generation has its own style of thought and action
— an idiom evident in the words it uses, the questions it asks,
the answers it finds. This is no less true of the Christian community than of any other. Today theologians find themselves writing more often and more extensively than ever
before about paintings, music, poetry, drama, and the novel.
Christians have never been able to ignore the arts, for music
and liturgy are allied. Poetry and drama have provided opportunities to convey the gospel. Theology, whatever else it
may be, is a literary discipline, and men must always be
warned against the temptation to make art their religion.

But the traditional attitude of the church displayed a more
or less constant rhythm. The arts were valued because they
were useful. The artist was welcomed as a servant of the
institution, although not as someone whose vocation had its
own claim to serious theological attention. On the other hand,
interest in iconography was balanced by a polemical spirit,
especially on Protestant soil. Part of the legacy of the Old
Testament was the knowledge that the lure of beauty could
be a snare:

You shall not make for yourself a graven image, or any likeness
of anything that is in heaven above, or that is in the earth beneath,

or that is in the water under the earth; you shall not bow down
to them or serve them. (Ex. 20:4-5.)

With the advent of romanticism, the old relationship was
altered. Art and religion made common cause against the
interpretation of man and the world as mechanisms, devoid
of spontaneity and creativeness. Sometimes religion seemed
reduced to poetry, but at least this was accompanied by a
new sense of the importance of the poet. " More and more,"
wrote Matthew Arnold, " mankind will discover that we
have to turn to poetry to interpret life for us, to console us,
to sustain us. Without poetry, our science will appear incomplete." [1] Sometimes poetry seemed to supplant religion, but at
least this meant an acknowledgment of aspects of life that
the logic of the sciences could not grasp. Faced with the development of Biblical criticism, romanticism insisted that the
Bible was not a textbook of primitive science but a kind of
poetry that answers ineradicable needs of the human spirit.
Men like Coleridge and Arnold were aware of affinities between religion and art which the traditional attitude of the
church had never recognized.

In 1882, Nietzsche completed *The Joyful Wisdom,* in
which he told his parable of the death of God. A madman
rushes into a village marketplace and cries, " Where is God? "
The villagers have long since ceased to believe, so they
laugh and suggest that God has gone on a voyage or emi-
grated to some foreign land. The madman feels the world
become colder and sees " night and more night coming on all
the while." Despite its antecedents in romanticism, contemporary theological concern with the arts is a new adventure.
Nietzsche has left his mark on it. It has been inspired by intellectual currents peculiar to the twentieth century. These
have shaped it in decisive ways. Part of its significance lies

in the assumptions on which it is predicated.

One of them is that religion is a journey as well as an arrival. It can be defined not only in terms of cult and ritual but also as a search for whatever sources of meaning and value there are for human life, and as an attempt to relate more satisfactorily to them. An existential interpretation of religion renders it possible to see religious options avowed and rejected in all forms of cultural activity, especially in imaginative literature and some painting. Life is not a bundle of fragments, one of which is religion. It is a unity, because we who live it are unitary creatures. If the artist is concerned with the ultimate source of meaning and value only in an indirect and implicit way, what he affirms still requires theological attention and deserves hearing within the religious establishment.

Another assumption concerns the necessity to relate the Christian message to the contemporary situation. The gospel is not preached in a vacuum. It must be interpreted for particular people at a particular time and place. As Paul Tillich has said:

A theological system is supposed to satisfy two basic needs: the statement of the truth of the Christian message and the interpretation of this truth for every new generation. Theology moves back and forth between two poles, the eternal truth of its foundation and the temporal situation in which the eternal truth must be received.[2]

Beside the portrayals of the human condition that modern art offers to us, much Christian preaching seems superficial and littered with clichés. Its irrelevance testifies that the church has taken the full measure of neither man's health nor his disease. Many of the old prescriptions are not effective now. One cure for theological sterility may involve greater

attention to the artist's voice. For Tillich, art is important because of the access it affords to the contemporary spiritual
climate. It discloses the prevailing image of man, sometimes
because the artist himself is unconsciously determined by it,
sometimes in the context of a protest against its adequacy or
truth. In either instance, art provides an opportunity to learn
where people are.

The various tragedies that have struck at human commu-
ity in our time have contributed to a heightened sense of the
religious character of perennial artistic images. The material
of theology is also the stuff of the arts: myths of the stranger
and the voyager, of the exile and the penitent, images of
death and rebirth, intimations of transfiguration and resur-
rection, judgment and grace, innumerable soteriological symbols. Contemporary art is a persuasive argument that
Nietzsche's report of the death of God was premature. A recent essay on the theological dimensions of modern literature
had as its epigraph a phrase from *Dies Irae*, the great medieval hymn: *teste David cum Sybilla*.[3] But other writers have
examined the altered forms in which these symbols appear in
our novels and poetry. The nature of their transfiguration
provides a way to measure the distinctiveness of our present
situation in the context of the tradition we have inherited.
They are used in ways that deprive them of the richness of
their original meaning, although their survival also indicates
the continuity between our fears and expectations, values and
patterns of interpretation, and those of earlier generations.

But the conclusion of such a venture must be that we live
in an age of broken symbols, when once-hallowed religious
images have suffered attrition and lost much of their power
to grasp either heart or mind. If the Hebrew-Christian tradition still furnishes the themes and symbols from which art
is made, they often appear in curiously truncated form, hav-

ing lost their depth, relevant for the interpretation of the labyrinthine ways of the heart but not cogent for the portrayal of the absurd universe into which man has been thrown. T. S. Eliot's words have the ring of truth:

> What are the roots that clutch, what branches grow
> Out of this stony rubbish? Son of man,
> You cannot say, or guess, for you know only
> A heap of broken images, where the sun beats,
> And the dead tree gives no shelter, the cricket no relief,
> And the dry stone no sound of water.[4]

One cause of this attrition is a new scientific vision: man the creature of heredity and environment, the prey of psychological processes he is often helpless to dominate. Another is sociological change, the urban culture which seems to render the agrarian imagery of the Bible anachronistic, the mobility that eventually severs old ethnic and family and parish bonds, the new modes of working in a technological society that make the Christian concept of vocation seem anomalous. And there are many for whom the Christian message has been cheapened simply because it is such a familiar ingredient of their environment, its import compromised by every highway sign assuring that Jesus saves and every song that tells how we are loved by " The Man Upstairs." In his juxtaposition of religious affirmations and backyard gossip, Eliot presents in " The Waste Land " the reduction of heritage to convention by the relentless pressures of familiarity. A few years ago an American psychoanalyst commented that

contemporary man suffers from the deterioration and breakdown of the central symbols in modern Western culture. . . . What we find typically in our patients in this decade is that no symbols seem to have compelling power and meaning to grip them any

more — not " God " nor " father " nor the " stars and stripes." A
decade or so ago the symbols related to " competitive success "
and " love " did have power to grasp people and elicit their al-
legiance; but there is reason for believing that these symbols too
have lost their power. . . . This is a central aspect of the " empti-
ness " experienced by so many contemporary sensitive persons.
. . . They land in a symbolic vacuum.[5]

Art mirrors something of the prevailing interpretation of
man and his condition and shapes that of future generations.
So it has inevitably become a focus of theological concern as
we try to speak with greater relevance and discernment to the
cultural situation in which we find ourselves. The church is
encountering new and distinctive problems of communication. Some Christians are persuaded that there may be much
to learn from new modes of discourse in the arts. " In today's
cultural disarray," Amos N. Wilder writes:

The modern literary artist in particular has much to teach us bear-
ing on the rediscovery of meaning, the sifting of traditions, the
discernment of spirits, and the renewal of the word. The problem
of communication for the church today is no less urgent than
for the artist. Our elaboration of a new grammar and rhetoric
of faith and apologetic can learn much from the new discourse of
the poets.[6]

Still other theologians are concerned with what the artist
does because of the way contemporary philosophers have
often denied the validity of religious language. Because the
claims of such language are not subject to any satisfactory
kind of empirical verification, they have been said to possess
no significance at all. The challenge of linguistic analysis
has rendered all the more important the investigation that the
nineteenth century began into the resemblances between
theological discourse and the language of art and poetry.

The Christian community finds itself embarked on a new adventure today. Its concern with the arts has been born out of a passion for relevance, for it is of no avail to answer questions that no one is asking. The adventure has been midwifed by a sense of the unity of life and an interpretation of religion that recognizes its presence not only in churches but in every quest for the foundations of meaning and value. It has been given urgency because of our contemporary cultural disarray and the predicament of the broken symbol. Its justification lies in a deepened awareness that theology is not the queen of the sciences, but one form of cultural activity among many.

The theological enterprise is much more, or much less, than the repetition to generation after generation of timeless truths once delivered to the saints. Its substance remains the revelation of God in Jesus Christ, but every expression of that substance is shaped by the historical and cultural circumstances from which it emerges. Always it bears the traces of its human origin. The theologian has no transcendent perspective; nor do those to whom he speaks. If the Christian message is to kindle man's imagination, it must address him where he stands and not demand that he stand somewhere else in order to hear it. One task of the theologian is to relate his discipline to other modes of cultural activity, to the arts and sciences, to historical studies and linguistic analysis. Out of this dialogue there can develop greater sensitivity to the new questions that confront the contemporary Christian community. Perhaps there will emerge some new and more persuasive forms in which the substance of the gospel can be cast. Perhaps there will also come a renewed appreciation of the meaning and importance of the traditional religious prescriptions and vocabulary.

The factors that have inspired theological interest in the artist's venture today are many and diverse. There is little unanimity evident either in the conclusions at which those who are concerned with it arrive, or in the reasons they offer for their concern. But at least there is a certain measure of agreement that no definition of man is adequate if it ignores the time and passion he spends inventing melodies and telling stories and decorating the walls of his tent or house or cave. An integral part of any satisfactory answer to the question of man is that man is an artist. What does it mean, from the vantage point of Christian faith, that men compose music and write poetry and cover pieces of canvas with paint? What are the theological implications of the fact that man is an artist? The questions can be answered in very different ways. But our contemporary cultural situation has awakened the Christian community to the importance of asking the questions, finding some answers, and recognizing the significance of his creativeness if it is to achieve any definition of man at all.

THREE OPTIONS FOR A " THEOLOGY OF ART "

Many of the theologians who have found themselves writing on the arts have been content simply to initiate conversations between two forms of cultural activity. But others have attempted what might be called theologies of art: interpretations of the origin and nature of the artist's venture in the context of the Christian story about man, the world, and God. They have sought to develop a systematic perspective on what artists are doing, why they are doing it, and what it means. A theologian does not have some kind of privileged access to the meaning of painting or poetry, however. He knows no more about them than anyone else who is presumably neither a painter nor a poet. What he does possess are myths and symbols which, to the eyes of faith, illuminate the human

situation. The Biblical account of what God has done both
for and with man provides resources for the interpretation
of present experience, for what God has done he is doing
still. But there is no way to discover which of these images
are particularly appropriate for the appraisal of the creative
enterprise except in the course of dialogue with art and
artists.

Three distinctive accents appear in contemporary theologies of art, for there are three great themes involved in the
Christian message. There is the story of God the Creator,
who establishes and maintains an appropriate context for the
life of the creatures he has made. There is the account of the
sovereign God who comes to disclose his holiness and enact
judgment upon man at Calvary. There is the conviction that
the ultimate word from the Lord is not judgment but mercy,
not condemnation but acceptance, and that he who raised
Christ from the dead will bring all things to fulfillment in
his Kingdom. Faith in the Creator, the message of the cross,
hope for the consummation — every Christian interpretation
of the human venture is derived from one of these three per-
spectives. The whole gospel involves the affirmation of them
all. When one is ignored, the others are impoverished as well.
So the church struggled against Marcion, whose rejection of
the Creator vitiated his appreciation of the Redeemer, as well
as against Pelagius, whose understanding of the will and
work of the Creator seemed to render Calvary gratuitous.

But if the Christian finds that the images of creation, cross,
and consummation bring some clarity and coherence to the
ambiguity of experience, primacy will finally be awarded to
one of them. It will serve as the foundation for which the
others provide the upper stories. Which one should it be?
How should the others be related to the dominant motif?
Should the artist's venture be understood primarily in the

context of man's origin or his end, his creation or his redemption, with reference to the Creator or to the fulfillment
of all things in the Kingdom of God? Where can principles
of discrimination and standards of criticism be found, in
Genesis or in the gospel? Each of these images has furnished
the vantage point for a theology of art developed by some
contemporary Christian writers.

One option is represented by Paul Tillich, who gives radical expression to the traditional Protestant perspective. He
tells us that every age has its own characteristic style, disclosed nowhere else so powerfully as in its art. In that style,
the reigning interpretation of human nature and destiny is
crystallized. The examination of artistic style is incumbent
on anyone who would relate the gospel to the contemporary
situation. So Tillich has employed paintings and sculpture
and recent drama to buttress his particular analysis of the
crisis of our culture. But his work does not reflect only an
apologetic interest. He is equally concerned to appraise the
arts in the light of the message of the cross. As he wrote in
The Religious Situation:

We find self-transcendence in every time, openness to the eternal,
a hallowing of time; but on the other hand we see the appropria-
tion of the eternal, the self-sufficiency of time, the secularization
of the holy. There is a movement to and fro between self-transcendence and self-sufficiency, between the desire to be a mere ves-
sel and the desire to be the content, between the turning toward
the eternal and the turning toward the self. In this action and reaction we discern the religious situation.[7]

Either the finite will turn away from the infinite and claim
to be ultimate itself, or else it will be open to the infinite and
confess its own finitude. Either it will claim to have no judge
beyond itself, or it will accept the role of a servant, seeking

to be no more than a medium for the revelation of what is truly ultimate, the source and judge of all. These are the only alternatives: either — or. When Jesus accepts the way of the cross he sacrifices all he has and all he is in order to be transparent to ultimate reality. The symbol of the cross is the standard for the appraisal of all human activity: it expresses the proper relation between the relative and the absolute and so it also discloses the alienated condition of all men. In its light we are constrained to recognize our estrangement and its source in pride and unbelief.

Nicolas Berdyaev, the Russian philosopher of religion, is another writer who has profoundly influenced contemporary Protestant thought. He interprets the artist's venture in an eschatological context; the contrast between present slavery and the final freedom of the children of God is his principal refrain. Man, out of his imagination, can fashion new and better worlds. Aesthetic activity is a protest against all that jeopardizes human liberty in our time. For Berdyaev, the image of consummation connotes the destruction of this world and man's liberation from bondage to it more than the fulfillment of life as we know it now. He tells us that art is essentially a religious phenomenon, in the sense that its motivation is not a natural one: the origin of the creative impulse is man's yearning for a different world.

But the artist's venture is not only a disclosure of a thirst for redemption. It is also a pledge of the coming of the Kingdom of God, for it is a genuine participation in God's own creativeness. Born out of man's discontent with the present, creativity is an epiphany of his future and the proper vocation for one who is made in the image of the creative God. Christ is the Liberator. The gift he offers is freedom. He calls men to the exercise of their creative powers and all such activity is a contribution to the Kingdom. The artist is a paradigm of the redeemed or Christian man. His creativeness is a refutation of every sort of determinism. It testifies that under God the future can be shaped so that human life will be richer and more satisfying than in earlier times.

Jacques Maritain and other representatives of the Catholic tradition adopt an entirely different perspective. While Berdyaev emphasizes the protest involved in the artist's venture, these writers stress the other side of the coin. Painting and music and poetry are not evidence of man's longing for another realm but natural fruits of the human spirit, a kind of celebration of what the Creator himself has done. What the artist does is not a participation in divine creativity but a response to it. Aesthetic activity is inspired by the pleasure that finite and definite things afford man's senses. If it tells of human freedom, it also speaks of the importance of limits and constraint in rendering that freedom concrete. The arts testify to the " connaturality " of man and his environment. They tell us this world is, as Jake Barnes comments in *The Sun Also Rises,* " a good place to buy in."

Creation, cross, consummation: how shall the three be related in order to shed as much light as possible on what the artist does, why he does it, what it means? Which one should be the dominant motif in a Christian interpretation of the creative enterprise? What the artist does can be done well or ill. From which image or combination of them can principles of discrimination be derived? One theological standard by which to judge the validity of the different approaches of Tillich, Berdyaev, and Maritain is this: whichever image dominates their work, it is only one of the three great themes in the Christian story. It must be related to the others and expressed in a way that is congruent with what they imply. It must not entail any diminishing of their significance. Another standard concerns the correlation between theological commentary and the actual origins of the artist's venture and its contributions to the total human enterprise. The perils of distortion and irrelevance are insuperable when systematic perspective is purchased at the cost of genuine dialogue.

This is a theological essay about the arts, especially the work of the man of letters. The subsequent comments on the origins of aesthetic activity and its importance for the welfare of man are intended to furnish a foundation for a Christian interpretation of his work. The essay will not have been worth the writing if there is finally no real correlation between aesthetic theory and theological gloss. How fully do Tillich, Berdyaev, and Maritain achieve such correlation? What limits are there on the attempt to relate Christian thought and the artist's venture? How adequately do these theologians express the implications of the Christian story for the interpretation of culture? What has Protestant theology to learn from their successes — or their failures?

Creation? Cross? Consummation? Where should the theology of culture start?

THE SERVICE OF THE MAN OF LETTERS

What is it that the man of letters does? Why is he important? There are two directions which an interpretation of the creative enterprise can take. Either it can search for reasons why the arts are useful or else it can trace their importance to the respite they offer from all useful pursuits. Both ways lead to some of the truth. The trouble lies in the distinction itself. We live in a utilitarian age and tend to equate the value of things with their usefulness. The family that prays together, so our pragmatic evangelical spirits tell us, stays together. But every rigidly utilitarian perspective is vicious. It fosters a kind of seriousness that blinds us to the humanizing power of much that has no importance at all for the satisfaction of biological needs. So our lives are robbed of a certain element of spontaneity and style. We find refuge from this flattening of things in shabby pleasures that cannot claim our loyalty or interest for long and soon grow as wearisome as our utilitarian activities. Is not art necessary because it is gratuitous, important because it does nothing but adorn?

In a fine book, *Homo Ludens,* Johan Huizinga argues that the elemental motivation for cultural activity is simply man's instinct for play. Everything we do involves a certain amount of it. At its most sophisticated as well as in its primitive stages, the whole human enterprise betrays its presence. The urge to play inspires our technological innovations, our jurisprudence, our scientific advances, our ventures in philosophy. The impulse is adulterated but never lost, although nowhere else is it quite so evident as in the arts and especially in music.[8] Huizinga writes:

Even those activities which aim at the satisfaction of vital needs — hunting, for instance — tend, in archaic society, to take on the play-form. Social life is endued with supra-biological forms, in the shape of play, which enhance its value. . . . By this we do not mean that play turns into culture, rather that in its earliest phases culture has the play character, that it proceeds in the shape and the mood of play. In the twin union of play and culture, play is primary. It is an objectively recognizable, a concretely definable thing, whereas culture is only the term which our historical judgment attaches to a particular instance.[9]

In its pure form, play is, first of all, voluntary, an act of freedom. Since there is no utilitarian motivation for it, play can always be deferred. We never need to do it, except " to the extent that the enjoyment of it makes it a need." [10] Secondly, there is always an element of conflict or tension involved in it, a striving either to determine some issue or to win some victory. It can be a contest for something or a representation of something. And sometimes it is both, as when children play at war. Thirdly, play calls us away from ordinary life into a realm with rules all its own and definite boundaries in time and space. Its definitive characteristic is that

play is not " ordinary " or " real " life. It is rather a stepping out of " real " life into a temporary sphere of activity with a disposition all its own. Every child knows perfectly well that he is " only pretending," or that it was " only for fun." [11]

Homo Ludens is an affirmation of the human spirit and imagination, of the freedom and spontaneity that grace life. It teaches us not to exaggerate the utilitarian character of what we do and not to ascribe ultimate value to what is nourished and sustained simply by man's urge to play. But if play is deaf to every utilitarian demand, the service it renders man is nonetheless indispensable. Not only does it offer release from the pressures of vital needs; it is a means by which man is brought out of isolation into community.

It brings people to a common place, enforces upon them common rules, gives them a common aim. It is a school in which we can learn the importance and the requirements of life together, a way that children are prepared for the adult public world. Play teaches respect for form and limits, instills a sense of fairness, heightens and refines the competitive impulse and our creative instincts. It furthers the will of the Creator that men should live together in just and orderly community. Play is not neutral or trivial, something to which men can afford to respond with indifference. It is always dangerous when the pressure of utilitarian concerns causes us to forget its importance or when we abandon the demands of genuine play for some less exacting and less humanizing surrogate.

Huizinga is especially persuasive when he writes of the arts. Are they not useless, and yet invested with their own importance just because of that? Does not the creative impulse have a humble origin, nothing more than the desire to escape from daily cares? Does not the allure of the arts lie simply in colors and forms that delight the eye, and melodies that please the ear? What is art if not fantasy? There is an obvious difference between a painting of a landscape and the view of distant mountains through a window, between the world created in a novel and the one we inhabit most of the time.

The description of art as a kind of play is particularly appropriate and important. It calls attention to the real autonomy and integrity of the creative enterprise. The artist's venture is intent upon nothing beyond itself. It is the servant of nothing outside itself. It lives in a realm with rules all its own, and definite boundaries. It follows its own intrinsic laws of development and is deaf to any appeals from other quarters. Its products are not to be used, but enjoyed.

But Huizinga is also aware of the affinities between the arts and other forms of cultural activity. He manages to acknowledge the diversity within the human enterprise and yet recognize its more or less unitary character as well. Every kind of human endeavor shares some measure of the play impulse which is expressed most fully in what the artist does. So, while the idea of play affirms the independence of the artist's venture, it does not imply its isolation from all else. *Homo Ludens* serves to warn against any interpretation of aesthetic activity that divorces it from other aspects of the cultural process.

Life requires that man adapt himself to the world and adapt the world to his own purposes. He must know himself sufficiently to be his own master and know the world sufficiently to exercise mastery over it. Aesthetic activity is one element in man's response to this necessity. Its contribution is indispensable to his commerce with the world, to his communication with other selves, and to his knowledge of himself. The creative impulse is related not only to the desire to adorn life but also to the struggle to preserve it. Art is not pure play, devoid of consequences for " ordinary life." Without it, there would be no ordinary life. Why? The answer concerns the way that language gives us the world and the relation between apprehension and expression.

Words are the means that we have for communicating with each other. They enable us to venture out into society and escape from our solitude. But language does something else, and something more fundamental, before it serves as an instrument for communication with other persons. We have more than confused feelings and momentary impressions to share only because we have already employed the words at our command to think about the world. As Susanne Langer has phrased it:

The things we can say are in effect the things we can think. Words are the terms of our thinking as well as the terms in which we present our thoughts, because they present the objects of thought to the thinker himself. Before language communicates ideas, it gives them form, makes them clear, and in fact makes them what they are. Whatever has a name is an object for thought. Without words, sense experience is only a flow of impressions, as subjective as our feelings; words make it objective, and carve it up into *things* and *facts* that we can note, remember, and think about. Language gives outward experience its form, and makes it definite and clear.[12]

We are aware of much that we have no words to describe. But awareness of something and reflection about it are very different. We can think about only that which we can name.

The protean stuff of experience must be carved up and sorted out by language before it can be analyzed by the mind. Words transform the world into an object of thought, and place it at the disposal of the intellect. They render experience memorable, divide up the confused flow of sense perceptions into significant units, organize situations and emotions into coherent patterns, relate events in terms of cause and effect. On the ingredients of experience, language bestows concreteness and relative permanence. Then they can be brought forth from the private world and subjected to critical scrutiny in the public domain of shared experience.

One can be aware of a sense of oppression or disquiet, but only through some expressive activity, by naming as its cause some noise or itch or forgotten appointment, can that feeling enter the realm of consciousness and be dealt with there. The object of consciousness is not simply the feeling itself but also the word that separates it from other ones, gives it concretion and an identity of its own. Language is so much involved in the process that brings experience before the intellect that words themselves are always part of the stuff with which intellect works.

It would be wrong, indeed, to think of language simply as a kind of midwife who presides over the emergence of something into the world of the mind, because the image implies that the process is more antiseptic than it really is. Language has a creative or constitutive role to play as it fashions our impressions into intelligible form. The meanings and values that are inherent in our world do not simply lie out there waiting to ride some word into the presence of the intellect, " as leaves might be found in the back yard in Autumn, waiting to be raked into the compost heap." [13] The words we use shape the meaning and character our experience will possess. As Eliseo Vivas has written: " We do not mean through language what is there independent of our signs; we constitute it as we refer to it. But the world we grasp is truly the world, for us." [14]

It is well to remember that our words are alive, constantly in the process of change, subject in various ways to the vicissitudes of time and often the victims of corruption or disease. Our vision of things is conditioned, for better and for worse, by whatever impact our particular historical and cultural situation has exerted upon our words. This is one reason why language does not function in the way in which a good mirror reflects the human face. It alters, and with it so does the character of our commerce with the world. The world we see, and cherish or rebel against, is one that the linguistic activities of our fathers and grandfathers and contemporaries have shaped for us. And the anatomy of our language, as well as our vocabulary, determines how the world will appear. As that structure changes in small but significant ways, so does the structure of our experience.

This constitutive role of language as it brings intelligibility to our experience is properly an aesthetic affair. *Aisthēsis* describes a concern for particularity, for the whatness and individuality of the situations, emotions, and things we confront. There is an apparent inconsistency in writing of language as constitutive of the way the world appears to us and then identifying such linguistic usage with the apprehension of the particularity of things. But language is not constitutive in the sense that it imposes clarity upon experience without regard for its actual texture. It may not be a transparent medium through which we grasp the world in the way that God does, but it is an instrument of adaptation developed in the struggle to relate more satisfactorily to the environment. It is elaborated for the sake of our conversations with reality. Its purpose is to render that dialogue more coherent and sensitive. The world is there, stubbornly reminding us of its reality, quite apart from what we think about it. And that is sufficient reason why we must work at thinking about it well. But if our intellectual activity is not entirely creative, neither is it a passive affair. Apprehension and interpretation are always interwoven in our use of words. They are not two different activities, but inseparable aspects of a single venture.

But language does not really satisfy our passion for acquaintance with the world. Our common linguistic activity often blurs the actualities of experience more than it clarifies them. It does so for a variety of reasons. We are always in a hurry and have little time for reflection. Words may become hackneyed and stale and ambiguous. Sometimes we are frightened by that which a deeper contact with things threatens to reveal, and therefore deliberately choose obscurantism. However, since language is intrinsically incapable of providing us with the more subtle and discriminating contact with the world, other persons, and our own inner lives which we require, we supplement it with more sophisticated forms of aesthetic activity. Some men make the artifacts that we call works of art. They are created for many of the same reasons effective in the development of language. They initiate us more fully to the particularity of the things and situations we confront and the emotions we feel. We must have such knowledge, but language alone does not provide it. The principal service of works of art lies in their compensation for the deficiencies of the linguistic process in clarifying the inner life of man and mapping his world.

The reasons why art is indispensable for our common life can be phrased either from the perspective of the artist or from that of someone who reads, listens to, or looks at a work of art. In the first instance, the answer concerns the relation between apprehension and embodiment. Apprehension is unsatisfactory and incomplete apart from the embodiment of what we are trying to understand — " embodiment " meant to designate not only the process of creating a sculpture or a painting but also the making of a poem or a novel. Only through expression do we become fully conscious of what it is we are attempting to express. This expressive activity may be very primitive, no more than a sudden gesture. But the more portentous and complex whatever it is that concerns the self, the more intense and subtle the effort to express it must become. So it is that our expressive activity undergoes increasing intellectual modifications as we seek to grasp more profound and obscure dimensions of our experience.

Only when our attempts at expression reach the incarnate state we call art do they prove entirely satisfying. Not until then can all the possibilities that are involved be harvested in the commerce between man and the world. As Iredell Jenkins has written:

If the sudden insights that we gain in appreciation are not fastened and synthesized by being embodied, they are at best inchoate and fugitive. . . . Experience is incomplete, and sinks back into the blurred landscape of consciousness from which it momentarily emerged, unless it can fix itself in a definite and structured image.[15]

The embodiment of a creative impulse or intuition refines it, clarifies it, amplifies it. The integral relation between apprehension and incarnation, no matter how alien it seems to many who are not artists, provides a fundamental motivation for the creative enterprise.

In *The Principles of Art,* R. G. Collingwood wrote an imaginary dialogue with a painter in the course of which the artist says:

"One paints a thing in order to see it. People who don't paint, naturally, won't believe that; it would be too humiliating to themselves. They like to fancy that everybody, or at least everybody of refinement and taste like themselves, sees just as much as an artist sees, and that the artist only differs in having the technical accomplishment of painting what he sees. But that is nonsense. You see something in your subject, of course, before you begin to paint it (though how much, even of that, you would see if you weren't already a painter is a difficult question); and that, no doubt, is what induces you to begin painting; but only a person with experience of painting, and of painting well, can realize how little that is, compared with what you come to see in it as your painting progresses. . . . A good painter — any good painter will tell you the same — paints things because until he has painted them he doesn't know what they are like." [16]

Painting is not an activity that is undertaken after the experience that inspires it is already complete. The painting is integrally related to the fulfillment of the experience itself. It is a vital stage in the process of " seeing well." Only in the process of applying paint to canvas, only in the course of all the physical activities his art requires, only through the action of his wrists and fingers in laying on the brush, does an artist apprehend the density and particularity of what he is painting. Although Collingwood's words are perhaps irrelevant to some abstract art, they capture the intimacy of the relation between apprehension, expression, and embodiment.

Another answer to the question of the importance of the artist's venture, offered from the perspective of one who encounters a work of art, concerns the difference between ordinary experience and aesthetic apprehension. Objects that are deliberately devised to elicit aesthetic apprehension introduce us more profoundly to the nature of things than our usual commerce with the world does. Anything can become the focus of aesthetic apprehension; we can bestow rapt concentration upon the particularity of any individual object — a beloved face, a curiously twisted tree, the neon menace of a jukebox. But works of art differ from natural objects because they are deliberately designed to capture and hold our attention, as the ingredients of our physical environment are not.

Most of our ordinary traffic with things and other persons is cursory and ephemeral, motivated by questions of utility and pleasure, mired in stereotypes and conventions. We are forever confusing similarity and sameness. But a poem or a sculpture or a symphony offers itself to us in a singular fashion; the aesthetic object rigorously determines the nature of our response. Our attention is grasped more or less intransitively, transfixed by the particularity of this one thing. For the moment, we are not concerned with its usefulness or its importance or with any similarities it may have with other things, but only with its own engrossing whatness. We are not concerned so much with what it says as we are with what it is. In this encounter the work of art does not seem to point beyond itself to anything else. Its meanings are primarily immanent instead of referential.

The power of a painting or a poem to elicit such a response is relative to many things. It is conditioned by the level of aesthetic interest of a person at a particular place and time, by his education and innate sensitivity, as well as by the relative import and formal perfection of the object itself. But to a greater or lesser degree, aesthetic apprehension means " the intransitive apprehension of an object's immanent meanings and values in their full presentational immediacy." [17] Because it is devised to trap our attention in this fashion, the object is not swallowed up immediately in the evanescent stream of our perceptions. Its meanings and values remain relatively well defined components of our experience. Our gaze is captured by its own whatness and specificity. It resists our inveterate tendency to embroider it with our own fantasies and preferences. Unlike much of our ordinary experience, in this meeting we are constrained to see not what we would like but what is there.

Art presents us with aspects of the world and dimensions of human experience as they have been grasped by a person who has discriminating and creative talent. He has worked to clarify his vision of things. He has contributed more to his commerce with them and so he has derived more from them. When we read a novel or look at a painting, our experience is particularly intense and rewarding because in some measure it is a repetition of that of the artist himself. Much antipathy toward contemporary fiction and expressionist painting derives simply from our unwillingness to become acquainted with the depths of existence. We prefer to walk on the surfaces and shutter our eyes. To quote Collingwood again:

We " see more in " a really good picture of a given subject than we do in the subject itself. That is why, too, many people prefer what is called " nature " or " real life " to the finest pictures, because they prefer not to be shown so much, in order to keep their apprehensions at a lower and more manageable level, where they can embroider what they see with likes and dislikes, fancies and emotions of their own, not intrinsically connected with the subject.[18]

Sometimes what we gain from the artist's venture is a heightened awareness of the ways of the world. Sometimes it is a clarified vision of the ways the human heart responds to the world. But whichever emphasis dominates, it does not entirely exclude the other. A reigning aesthetic theory since the days of Croce has been that art is essentially the expression of emotion. The discursive symbolism of our common speech cannot very well express the nature of human courage or anxiety. We can say that we are afraid, but how life is

for a man gripped by fear, its lacerating psychic consequences, this our ordinary speech does not convey. The arts,
and especially music, portray the vital patterns of human
feeling and provide us with some sort of objective correlative
which gives us access to the shape and substance of our emotions. The service of the arts in rendering intelligible the
realm of feelings seems analogous to the function that concepts perform in the organization of our experience of the
external world. Mrs. Langer claims:

The primary function of art is to objectify feeling so that we can
contemplate and understand it. . . . Art objectifies the sentience
and desire, self-consciousness and world-consciousness, emotions
and moods, that are generally regarded as irrational because
words cannot give us clear ideas of them. . . . [But] the life of
feeling is not irrational; its logical forms are merely very different from the structure of discourse.[19]

The definition of art as the expression of emotion or the
presentation of forms of feeling, however, is not adequate.
It implies a kind of separation between subjective and objective, man and the world, that contradicts the actualities of
our experience. Emotions do not arise in a vacuum. They are
not arbitrary and capricious. We do not simply become angry, we become angry about something; we are not simply
discontented, our discontent has a cause. Feelings are elicited
by the character of our social and physical environment and
are shaped by our values and goals. A passion is the consequence of the impact the world has upon us, and it reveals, in
its own obscure and nonconceptual way, the nature of our
universe. Much of the finest painting of our time has been
concerned not with the world itself but with what it feels
like to live in the world. But still the import and character
of objective reality is grasped by the artist and offered to us
in and through these emotions it inspires. As Maritain re-

minds us, emotion has a certain cognitive value. It gives us
real access to things. Through it we see.

Most of us are not very well acquainted with the actual
origins and true nature of our feelings. Life allows us little
time to investigate these things. We have an ineradicable
tendency to repress the most frightening of them, to disguise
and embroider upon the shabbiest of our motivations and desires. We do it, first of all, not because we want to fool others.
We want to fool ourselves. The artist helps to introduce us
to who we are. He furnishes some part of the answer to the
old petition of the religious man: Help us to become the masters of ourselves so we might be the servants of others. Unless
we know ourselves well, unless we can grasp the range of our
feelings and comprehend their specificity, unless we can face
our motivations for what they are and correlate emotions
with the real factors that inspire them, we are not the masters
of our own house.

In Arthur Miller's *Death of a Salesman,* Willy Loman
mortgages his character as a moral agent because the exigencies of earning a salary compel him to orient his whole
life toward the ephemeral virtue of being well liked. Not
only because he is weak and foolish, but also because he must,
Willy lives for his image in the eyes of others. When one day
their gaze is averted, Willy's life is through. Miller portrays
a society that forces its members to be less concerned with the
self than with the image the self projects. His work has
formed part of the emotional response of many of us to the
contemporary civilization. He has brought us some clarity of
vision and a renewed awareness that cultural gods are jealous
gods: Moloch demands not burnt offerings but human sacrifice. The impact of *Death of a Salesman* is perhaps a small
instance of the truth mixed with hyperbole in Owen Barfield's comment, " There is a very real sense, humiliating as

it may seem, in which what we generally call *our* feelings are really Shakespeare's ' meaning.' " [20]

In this world, we encounter a baffling conglomeration of things, people, and situations. In ourselves we discover an equally baffling conglomeration of feelings. We are interested in what all these are, in what kinds of relationships exist among them, and in what their meaning and value are for ourselves. We are necessarily concerned with the particularity, the connectedness, and the import of the ingredients of our experience. In *Art and the Human Enterprise,* Iredell Jenkins defends the claim that

aesthetic activity is a natural and spontaneous phase of man's ordinary response to the environment; that it is a necessary partner in the process of adjustment; that art exists for life's sake, and that life could not exist without art.[21]

He argues that there are different appetites of the consciousness which focus our attention on these three dimensions of things. These orientations are all coordinate in status, equally necessary to the adaptive process. When one of them fails to function as it should, our grasp of the world is distorted and becomes inadequate. Then the whole human venture is threatened.

But the aesthetic component of psychic activity, Jenkins tells us, actually fails to apprehend the specific character of what we confront. Life affords almost insuperable passive resistance to the aesthetic quest for particularity because of the constant pressure of biological needs. So our glimpses of particularity are blurred and casual and fleeting. The distinction between appearance and reality, illusion and truth, is too subtle and too important to be surrendered to the tyranny of habits, conventionality, and worn axioms. But that is what really happens most of the time. When we do not know what things are in themselves, however, we have no perceptive vision of how they are related to one another or what their significance and value are. So we must find a way to compensate for the inadequacy of this mode of consciousness. We find it in the artist's venture. Life requires art. The motivation for the creative enterprise is ultimately a pragmatic one. " In the final analysis," Jenkins contends,

all creativity has a pragmatic basis: it is initiated and continued in order to improve the quality of man's transactions with the environment, to extend and refine his grasp of things, and to permit him to come to grips with the world more effectively.[22]

Man's aesthetic appetite is irrepressible. It must be satisfied if the human venture is to survive. But most of us cannot satisfy it for ourselves. We are dependent on other agencies to do so for us. We need not look to the arts, however. The question that especially concerns Jenkins is whether our hunger for the particularity of things will be answered well or ill, by authentic creativity or by the pseudo art that proliferates in every culture but with quite extraordinary rapidity in our own.

If we remain indifferent to the aesthetic education of our culture — if we do not care under what distorted and unrealistic guises particularity is presented to us — we cannot be surprised at the aberrant values men place upon things, the false expectations of life that they entertain, and the crushing disillusionments that they encounter. These errors and failures are inevitably laid up for them when their encounters with actual particulars have been prepared by a pseudo art that peoples their familiarity and their anticipations with things that never were and never could be.[23]

Apprehension, interpretation, expression, embodiment — these are organically related to one another. The creation of a work of art is the normal outcome of experience, not a bit of *exotica*. But the impulse to create is ordinarily thwarted in our lives, if it reaches the level of consciousness at all, partly because the exigencies of our daily concerns allow little time for it, partly because we are usually content with casual and conventional experience. Few of us are often arrested by any compulsion to look at things in the meticulous way a good painter or novelist does. Perhaps most of the time we do not need to award the world such scrupulous attention as artists do. But we will turn somewhere to increase our knowledge of the particularity of things. If we do not find good ways to supplement our own vision, we will inevitably depend on bad ones: hack magazine illustrators and shabby films, mindless jukeboxes, the vicious stereotypes that find perennial habitation in our common speech, the phony slogans that offend Holden Caulfield in *The Catcher in the Rye,* and television programs that pander to the most coarse and superficial taste. If there is no vital art at hand to clarify the nature of things, we will find substitutes for it, whether consciously or not, in what Jenkins labels pseudo art.

In some ways *Art and the Human Enterprise* is not persuasive. The motives that impel men to paint or write are too various and complex to sustain the claim that all creativity has a pragmatic basis. The artist's venture is a kind of play. Sometimes it is initiated simply because men have a desire to spin a galaxy of possible worlds out of their unfettered imagination, sometimes because they have an obscure but ineradicable ambition to image their emotions on canvas or on the stage, sometimes just because certain colors, forms, and sounds are, in themselves, pleasant to see or hear.

The word " pragmatic " obscures the autonomy of the creative enterprise, for it implies that art is really inspired by some nonaesthetic ends and is important because of its instrumental value. The Greek word for truth is *alētheia,* which means that something is disclosed or unveiled. So it is with the nature of our world, which is unveiled and organized for us through the symbolic process that eventually leads to the arts. Because we cannot understand their import or connectedness until we grasp the whatness of things, the artist's venture is invested with vital significance. But this value is derived from the character of *aisthēsis* as disinterested perception, a mode of consciousness concerned with nothing except particularity for its own sake. Art serves us precisely because it is intent on nothing beyond itself, deaf to all questions about its own utility, in search of particularity not because such knowledge is useful but because of its intrinsic appeal.

But all of us need to be reminded that it is the artist who is the creator of culture. His work shapes our feelings, our loyalties, our goals. The books and magazines we read, the television programs and films we watch, the music we hear, and the advertisements we believe — these determine our visions of ourselves and of our world. Artists grind the lenses through which society will look to understand man's nature and possibilities. They legislate the values that are the legacy of one generation to the next. The process is reciprocal, of course; the artist is no less influenced by his time and culture than the housewife or theologian. But the loyalties that gradually evolve in the course of our experience are shaped by the art with which our parents, our friends, and ourselves are acquainted. It is no small thing if we harvest our interpretations and expectations of life not from genuine art but from substitutes which present us with sentimentalized or idealized versions of existence that suppress its profound ambiguity, pander to our dreams and frailties, and so offer spurious comfort and false security.

Art is also creative of culture in the sense that it discloses the values actually operative in our society and the factors which are really at work in determining our response to the world but which we have been unable to grasp by ourselves or have deliberately chosen to ignore. Artists not only shape society, they bring to its members the possibility of some critical awareness of its true character. Furthermore, life does not stand still; new threats and opportunities constantly emerge. The artist serves to acquaint us with change, so we can respond to new challenges and not confuse them with old opportunities with which we were long since familiar. He is one figure, if not the only one, who presides over the birth of these new options as effectual forces in the cultural process. Writing on poetry, Vivas comments:

Once a poem is assimilated individually or culturally, its readers get the impression that its object imitates meanings and values with which they have been more or less well acquainted all along. But this is an illusion. For the values and meanings of a culture are never known, or never known clearly, or never known in their full density and specificity by those who participate in the culture until the poem reveals them. . . . Because poetry exercises an influence on the values actualized in a culture it has a normative function to perform. Thus to the extent that the poet succeeds in revealing meanings and values which are actually involved in an emergent sense in the social process, he becomes the creator of culture and the meanings and values thus revealed become constitutive of culture.[24]

The conventional distinction between art and life rests on the assumption that the artist is concerned with beauty, not with truth. The distinction is not only invidious, it is quite irrelevant to the venture of the man of letters. If the truth the artist seeks is different from what philosophers and scientists try to find, it is no less truth because of that. The artist is concerned with *a* world, the philosopher and the scientist with *the* world. They are concerned with the universal, the artist with the particular. The artist portrays one of the many worlds of human experience in all of its density and specificity. He knows the world and presents it to us in and through the emotions that existence in it elicits. They attempt to express the nature of things in abstraction from the passions the world arouses. The philosopher is concerned with concepts, the artist's stuff is symbols and images. The philosopher argues at the bar of logic. The meaning of art resides not only in its intelligible sense but also in the form and style and images, in sonority and cadence and the phonological structure of the language itself. But a work of art is still a cognitive penetration of reality.

The world a novel offers us is fashioned at the price of selectivity and exaggeration, though replete with its own logic and order. In this world we are initiated to the particularity of things and situations which, to our jubilation or dismay, comprise our own world as well. Now they are caught in structured and enduring images. But the novel also offers us some of the emotional responses such a world would elicit from its inhabitants. The writer presents us not only with one conceivable world but also with a report of what it would feel like to live in it and be motivated by the same factors that inspire the populace of his fiction. Insofar as these emotions are or illuminate our own, to that further extent the world that the artist has created is one in which we live, no matter how much fantasy and exaggeration it contains. His work becomes an instrument that enables us to grasp the actual character of our own feelings, the logic behind them, their relationship to situations, values, and goals which, whether hitherto recognized or not, motivate our actions.

But the services of the man of letters cannot finally be measured in terms of the clarified vision he offers us through his work. It is not the truth his novels and poetry convey that

matters most of all. It is what he does with language. The
world is there. We did not put it there. But words make it
what it is for us. Language evolves in the course of our struggle to bring some coherence and clarity to the confusion of
our experience. The quality and the comprehensiveness of our
vocabulary determine the quality and the scope of the world
our minds can grasp and to which our sensitivity can respond.
Every generation has a store of linguistic capital which it has
inherited. But this legacy must have its guardians, for language is alive and no less vulnerable than all other things to
the ravages of time.

> Words strain,
> Crack and sometimes break, under the burden,
> Under the tension, slip, slide, perish,
> Decay with imprecision, will not stay in place,
> Will not stay still. Shrieking voices,
> Scolding, mocking, or merely chattering,
> Always assail them.[25]

If language is to shape a world that can claim honest loyalties, a world instinct with meaning and value, then words
constantly need to be redeemed from coarse and superficial
usage, saved from the attrition that deprives them of their
wealth of connotations, rescued from the ambiguity that blurs
and blunts their meanings, honed to a sharp edge so they can
trap significance again. Unless these things are done and well
done, conversations will be made only

Out of the slimy mud of words, out of the sleet and hail of verbal
imprecisions.[26]

Not only man but also man's language is a soteriological
problem. Words need to be saved. That is what the man of
letters does. This is the heart of his venture and the requisite

for every truly human venture. Few men have been able to phrase the vocation of the artist in as eloquent and seminal a fashion as Allen Tate. In *The Man of Letters in the Modern World,* he wrote:

It is the duty of the man of letters to supervise the culture of language, to which the rest of culture is subordinate, and to warn us when our language is ceasing to forward the ends proper to man. The end of social man is communion in time through love, which is beyond time.[27]

Caught in the midst of empty formalities and irrelevant platitudes, banal words and stale images, we can never escape our solitude. These are the real agents, all the slogans that subsume what is particular and individual beneath some stereotype, which divorce us from reality and from one another as well. At the heart of much contemporary theater, there is a lacerating awareness of the way our common speech can come apart at the seams, until life itself is all unstitched. In Eugène Ionesco's *The Bald Soprano,* four characters talk at one another, but never with:

" I'll give you my mother-in-law's slippers if you'll give me your husband's coffin."
" I'm looking for a monophysite priest to marry to our maid.". . .
" The car goes very fast, but the cook beats batter better.". . .
" Charity begins at home."
" I'm waiting for the aqueduct to come and see me at my windmill."
" One can prove that social progress is definitely better with sugar."
" To hell with polishing."
" One doesn't polish spectacles with black wax."
" Yes, but with money one can buy anything."
" I'd rather kill a rabbit than sing in the garden." [28]

As the curtain falls, the torrent of *non sequiturs* has become only a meaningless agglomeration of consonants and vowels, sound and fury signifying nothing at all. To name our malady, to show how words can obscure instead of clarify, erode community instead of create it, is scarcely to cure the disease. But it is one step toward health renewed, the first service of the man of letters in redeeming our words.

There are some particular ways the germs of dissolution can enter the fiber of a language, and particular ways that the artist's venture provides an antidote for such infection. But at this juncture it is enough to establish the claim that art is not *exotica,* some rare flower that mysteriously appears in the middle of a vegetable garden. It inevitably develops from the character of the human situation. The fundamental aspect of that situation is simply that experience is confused and needs to be sorted out. We accomplish this through our aesthetic activity, which is no less important if we are to adapt to the world than is technology if we are to adapt the world to our own purposes.

We discover the world through creative acts. Only in the course of some expressive act do we grasp the exact nature of whatever it is that we are struggling to express. Our means of expression are all interpretive devices. Language is not a window through which intellect looks at experience; it carves up and organizes experience so intellect can look at it. Words are not little carts that draw experience up to the mind's house; they transform it into the kind of stuff with which mind can work. The words we have are alive. Time disperses their meaning and we use them in ways that vitiate their power to serve us. Their redemption is important because it means the redemption of the way the world appears to us.

Language is the principal instrument that man uses to satisfy his aesthetic appetite for the particularity of things, although it is not an entirely adequate instrument. Our common linguistic activity often blurs the actuality of our experience. But the pressure of our daily tasks allows us little time to attend to the actual character of situations and emotions. We are always in a hurry and suspect that it really does not matter if we confuse similarity and sameness. So the vague impulse to give some kind of greater permanence to our intimations of the nature of the world remains unfulfilled. But still we hunger for a more subtle and discriminating acquaintance with particularity and a more sensitive contact with the world, with other selves, and with our own inner lives.

Some men offer us more sophisticated forms of aesthetic activity than we can provide for ourselves. They give us poems and paintings and novels. Life would not have it otherwise. The human venture depends on what they do. If we are not schooled in the whatness of things by honest and perceptive men, we will accept some counterfeit coin. We will get our education somewhere. Our own perceptions are too slender to do without supplement, our hunger for ampler vision too strong.

Art is a kind of play, endowed with its own autonomy and independence. But it is an impure expression of the play impulse, because it is integrally related to our ordinary lives. It emerges by an intrinsic necessity from man's relation to his world. The venture of the man of letters is of particular importance, for he guards and renews the words that place things at the disposal of our intellects. These are the principal claims with which this essay on the arts is concerned. But theological commentary on them must be postponed until we have examined the three distinctive options that have developed in this new adventure, the theology of art.

II

PAUL TILLICH AND THE
MESSAGE OF THE CROSS

THE DEFENSE OF RELIGION

In 1799, Friedrich Schleiermacher published *On Religion: Speeches Addressed to Its Cultured Despisers*. It heralded a new era in Protestant thought, for Schleiermacher did not attempt to justify Christianity and its dogmas. In a time of hostility and indifference toward it, his concern was to defend religion itself as an integral dimension of human life. The vindication of religion, especially in the face of advances in scientific knowledge and method, was a characteristic nineteenth-century venture. Paul Tillich stands in this tradition. His message is that religion and culture are integrally related. When the human enterprise disavows its religious dimension, its fate is bankruptcy and meaninglessness, for

no realm of life can exist without relation to something unconditional, to an ultimate concern. Religion, like God, is omnipresent; its presence, like that of God, can be forgotten, neglected, denied. But it is always effective, giving inexhaustible depth to life and inexhaustible meaning to every cultural creation.[1]

Among contemporary Protestant theologians who explore the relation between religion and culture, no one has exerted such influence as Tillich, particularly in America. From the New Testament, he extracts the idea of " transparency," and this is the standard by which he appraises the human enterprise. The same norm is expressed by the Protestant Principle, derived from man's intuitive recognition of an unconditional and ultimate element in human life. When it is elaborated as an interpretation of the world, the Protestant Principle becomes " self-transcendent naturalism." As an attitude toward the world, it entails " belief-ful realism." Its historical realization is "theonomy," which designates a situation in which the autonomous aspirations of culture are transcended in an orientation toward what sustains and judges contingent being. What all these affirm is that the meaning of the world lies in its capacity to become a medium for the manifestation of ultimate reality. This potentiality is normatively expressed by the cross of Christ. Men must be brought to acknowledge the unconditional element that sustains and consecrates all significant activity, while their demonic claims to have no judge beyond themselves must be challenged in the name of what is truly ultimate.

In 1919, Tillich wrote " Über die Idee einer Theologie der Kultur." He argued that religion must not be defined as commerce with supernatural beings or ritual activities or the acceptance of certain dogmas, but rather as " inner direction toward the Unconditioned." [2] To be religious is to be unconditionally concerned, no matter how secular the fashion in which this concern is expressed.[3] As ultimate concern, religion is a pervasive ingredient in life, manifest in morals as an awareness of the unconditional seriousness of the moral demand, in the aesthetic realm as the desire to articulate ultimate meaning, in the cognitive sphere as the passion for ultimate truth. To repudiate religion for moral or aesthetic or intellectual reasons is to repudiate it in its own name. Religion cannot be rejected with ultimate seriousness because that is what it means: unconditional concern with self and world, their estrangement and finitude and ultimate significance.

Where there is ultimate concern, God can be denied only in the name of God. . . . Ultimate concern cannot deny its own character as ultimate. Therefore, it affirms what is meant by the word "God." . . . Indifference toward the ultimate question is the only imaginable form of atheism. . . . He who denies God as a matter of ultimate concern, affirms God, because he affirms ultimacy in his concern.[4]

Tillich's existential interpretation of religion precludes the divorce of religion and culture that has so often characterized Protestant thought and made its pronouncements abstract and irrelevant. Every distinction between the two is tentative and provisional. No longer is religion a special aspect of the human enterprise or particularly associated, in the fashion of Schleiermacher or Ritschl, with a single psychic function. It is present everywhere, for the implicit presupposition of all activity is something unconditional that sustains finite meanings above the void of meaninglessness. So Tillich claims that religion is the substance of culture, culture the form of religion.[5]

Tillich does not mean that religion is a subjective affair. He stands more or less in the tradition of Augustine, Bonaventure, and medieval mysticism, convinced that "man is immediately aware of something unconditional which is the prius of the separation and interaction of subject and object, theoretically as well as practically."[6] He stresses the immediate, intuitive, and noninferential character of such awareness. This element of ultimacy never appears as the content of experience. It is the prius of every experience. As James Luther Adams has phrased it:

This unconditional element is recognized in and beyond all absolutely serious concerns, in all logical and aesthetic, in all legal and social, action. In all these meaningful activities there appears not only a definite concrete meaning but also a sense of the meaningfulness of the whole, the unity of all possible meanings. But more than a totality of meaning is involved, for a mere totality of meaning could sink into a void of meaninglessness. In the totality of meaning there lives an unconditional meaning which is itself not a meaning but rather the basis of meaning. This is the unconditional element in all being and meaning.[7]

Ultimate concern becomes explicit whenever a man is suddenly grasped and shaken by the unconditioned ground of all meaning and being, and constrained to respond with absolute seriousness to the moral or aesthetic or cognitive dimensions of life. But Tillich insists, in the fashion of Kant, that this ontological intuition cannot be transformed into an argument for the existence of God. The element of ultimacy involved in human life does not justify talk about a highest being or another world beyond the world of time and space.[8]

If this awareness of ultimate reality is absolutely certain, it is not truly cognitive. Man is grasped by what precedes the distinction between self and other, by what infinitely transcends the subject-object polarity on which human knowledge is based. So the way this experience is conceptualized is a matter of contingency and risk. The contingent element is the constellation of myths and symbols through which the ontological intuition becomes sufficiently concrete to be an object of direct concern. The particular symbols in which it is expressed are determined by one's time and place. These symbols are the stuff with which theologians work.[9] Theology is the normative aspect of the philosophy of religion. Its task is to interpret and criticize religious symbols. They render concrete the object of ultimate concern, but they also threaten to deprive it of its ultimacy.[10]

The standard for the theological venture is implied in the

ontological awareness itself: what is unconditional must not be conditioned, nor what is relative made absolute. In the history of religion, many symbols have idolatrously been identified with what they were intended to symbolize. Many beings and powers have been regarded as though they were ultimate. But there has always been a critical principle at work, guarding the integrity of what is truly ultimate. This is the Protestant Principle. It must not be confused with the historical reality of Protestantism, which stands under its judgment.[11] The Protestant Principle points toward the depth of things, toward what sustains every conditioned meaning and being but which not even the totality of finite meanings can exhaust. So it affirms the world in the name of what is unconditional insofar as the world is transparent and " the ultimate meaning of existence shines through all finite forms of thought and action." [12] But it also means the denial of every pretension of the conditioned to possess unconditional power and authority, of every instance of imperialism whether sacred or secular, of every absolute claim launched by what is relative. " It is the guardian against the attempts of the finite and conditioned to usurp the place of the unconditional in acting and thinking." [13]

OUR KNOWLEDGE OF GOD

Tillich departs from traditional patterns of Protestant thought in a radical fashion when he insists that God neither is, nor is known as, " Other." As a symbol for what concerns man ultimately, " God " designates what precedes or underlies the self-other and subject-object polarities. The inadequacy of all supernaturalism lies in the way it subordinates God to the categories of finitude. He is relegated to a realm above or beyond this world. He must confront his creatures from a distance. He is only one being among many beings, even though the greatest. So the ultimate is deprived of its ultimacy, for " in every ' above ' lies a ' beside ' and in every ' beside ' a ' conditioned.' " [14] Because it is content to place God beside the finite, traditional theism severs religion and culture, divides loyalty, destroys the unity of life. Against it, the protest of naturalism is always valid, for " what stands ' beside ' is by reason of this very position a single, finite meaning, for which one would then have to seek a basis of meaning, a God over God, a religion over religion." [15] Naturalism is a kind of obscure witness to the ultimacy of what is ultimate. Christianity must " accept the antisupranatural criticism of naturalism." [16]

But naturalism errs as much as theism, for it denies the inexhaustible character of the source of meaning and being. Both options are impossible. As an alternative, Tillich proposes self-transcendent or ecstatic naturalism. " Self " involves an acknowledgment of the limits of knowledge. God is not a cognitive object.[17] " Transcendent " expresses the separation of the finite from its unconditioned ground. God

stands *against* the world, in so far as the world stands against him, and he stands *for* the world, thereby causing it to stand for him. This mutual freedom from each other and for each other is the only meaningful sense in which the " supra " in " supranaturalism " can be used. Only in this sense can we speak of transcendent with respect to the relation of God and the world. . . . The finite world points beyond itself.[18]

Pantheism is impossible not because there is some incontrovertible argument for a highest being, nor on grounds of special revelation, but because men are free.[19]

Theology is the description of the human condition with reference to its ultimate meaning, a protest against the absolutist pretensions of what is relative and a portrayal of the power of all things to point "beyond themselves and their finite existence to the infinite, inexhaustible, and unapproachable depth of their being and meaning." [20] It is an existential affair from which no assertions can be extracted concerning God in and for himself, for that would require "a supernaturally authoritative revelation, but that concept has been overcome by the wave of religious-historical insights and the logical and religious criticism of the conception of supernaturalism." [21] The proper business of theology is not to discuss

the nature and attributes of God, enriching or restricting the traditional statements, but rather it is its task to contemplate the real in such a way that its divine ground becomes transparent in it and through it. The profoundest demand of all is that we learn to speak of God in such a way that he appears not as an object above all other objects, nor as a mere symbol, but as the really real in everything that claims reality. [22]

Except for the assertion that he is Being-Itself, all language about God is symbolic or analogical. [23] Religious symbols are independent of empirical criticism, not vulnerable to the discoveries of the natural sciences or historical research. [24] But there are two criteria by which to judge them: objectively, they must not be demonic; subjectively, they must be adequate. [25] If they are not to be demonic, they must convey their own contingent character, as well as the contingency of all being. They must contain an element of self-negation: "All idolatry is nothing else than the absolutizing of symbols of the Holy, and making them identical with the Holy itself." [26]

The other criterion is more elusive. The subjective validity of symbols "is their adequacy to the religious situation in which they are created and their inadequacy to another situation is their untruth." [27] When a symbol has somehow been reduced to a sign, so that its relation to ultimate reality seems merely arbitrary and conventional, it has become inadequate and is therefore untrue.[28] The only claim of religious discourse to meaning and truth would seem to be one phrased in terms of expressive power. So the cognitive value of religious symbols is negligible.

Then how is it possible to decide which of different interpretations of God is most satisfactory? Does the significance of these symbols lie wholly in their evocative power? Tillich writes that symbols " participate " in what they symbolize; for instance, " the flag participates in the power and dignity of the nation for which it stands." [29] The illustration suggests that participation simply designates the more vivid way symbols grasp the imagination than conventional and arbitrary signs can do. But for the Christian tradition, the validity of religious language has never rested upon its expressive power. The symbols have been important because of the knowledge about God that Christians believed they conveyed. Whatever power they have possessed to grasp and shake a person has been derived from their efficacy as conveyors of knowledge. As one of Tillich's critics has said:

An earnest religious individual wants to know the divine reality, and yet, his earnestness is not a sufficient condition for selecting true beliefs from other beliefs which may be held with equal earnestness. Earnestness is a condition for learning but it is not a criterion by which the character of belief can be ascertained. According to religious faith, the criterion for the truth-character of interpretations of the divine reality is a knowledge of the divine reality.[30]

Nevertheless, Tillich argues that the Biblical picture of the Christ is " final " revelation. It is decisive. He is able to claim this because, for him, the New Testament witness to the Christ is comprehensively expressed by the symbol of the cross. This one event captures the whole meaning of the life and work of Jesus.[31] It escapes the demonic ambiguity of symbols and perfectly fulfills the objective criterion of the truth of faith. Christianity transcends all other forms of religion because the cross is a symbol that contains an unsurpassable element of self-negation.[32]

If Christianity claims to have a truth superior to any other truth in its symbolism, then it is the symbol of the cross in which this is expressed. . . . He who himself embodies the fullness of the divine's presence sacrifices himself in order not to become an idol, another god beside God, a god into whom the disciples wanted to make him. And therefore the decisive story is the story in which he accepts the title " Christ " when Peter offers it to him. He accepts it under the one condition that he has to go to Jerusalem to suffer and to die, which means to deny the idolatrous tendency even with respect to himself. This is at the same time the criterion of all other symbols.[33]

Symbols are mortal. They are born and they die. But the cross eludes the laws of finitude that govern all others, for

it has the power of negating itself without losing itself. This paradox is based on the fact that every revelation is conditioned by the medium in and through which it appears. The question of the final revelation is the question of a medium of revelation which overcomes its own finite conditions by sacrificing them, and itself with them.[34]

The medium of this revelation claims nothing for himself. So he is wholly revelatory, transparent to the ground of meaning and being. This is final revelation, " universal without being heteronomous," because " no finite being imposes itself in the name of God on other finite beings." [35] Christian thought is concerned not with the historical Jesus but with the Biblical picture of the crucified Messiah. "Jesus is the religious and theological object as the Christ and only as the Christ . . . as the one who sacrifices what is merely 'Jesus' in him." [36]

This revelation perfectly fulfills the subjective criterion of religious symbolism, for its expressive power is not limited to a particular time or place or religious tradition. The cross points toward the ultimacy of what is ultimate without advancing any claims at all on behalf of what is contingent and relative. The whole problem of the culturally conditioned and historically relative character of the New Testament has simply disappeared.[37] The story of the crucifixion offers a symbol through which the ontological awareness presupposed by every form of religious faith can become concrete without any distortion or loss of purity at all. In the idea of transparency it provides a norm universally applicable.

Tillich's interpretation of the Christ is far too subtle and complex to be examined so briefly.[38] But for him the cross is no more than the normative symbol for the expression of an intuition antecedently and universally available. Revelation does not contribute anything to the theology of culture that is not already available on the basis of the ontological certainty itself. The fundamental problem is that the Bible is dissolved into this single meta-historical image. So the Old and the New Testament are deprived of their historical character. They are no longer witnesses to a God who wills to participate in the human situation and who constantly assumes the initiative in all his transactions with man. Does the interpretation of the cross in terms of transparency to ultimate reality mean that the Christ event can still be called an act of God? One critic of the Christology of Tillich has written:

In this view, the God of theism, the God who has been adored in all religions and who, as it was hitherto believed by Christians, revealed himself in Jesus the Christ, is only a convenient source of concrete symbols for a philosophical theory concerning the " power to be." . . . The myth of the Cross is a convenient image for the death of the God of theism and his replacement by the power to be.[39]

The criticism does no justice to Tillich. But it is plausible because of the one element which his Christology so notably lacks. However various their persuasions about other things, Christians have been united by their faith that Christ represents the supreme instance of deliberate divine volition in all history. But as Tillich interprets the gospel, it is doubtful whether one can speak of divine volition or purpose at all. He is skeptical of such language because of its involvement with traditional theism. It implies that God is outside the world and then determines to come into it. It implies that he is somewhere outside of nature rather than the power of being that sustains all things. It implies that his relations with the world are external and transitive. It reduces him to the status of one being among the many beings of the universe.

But the loss far exceeds the gain, if one cannot speak without ambiguity of divine decision, volition, will, and initiative. Does God will the existence of that which is other than himself? Does he will to maintain it in its distinction from himself in order that it might attain the fulfillment appropriate to its creaturely nature? Is creation an act of love? Or is it a fall from some higher unity? How one answers these questions is crucial for the theology of culture. The standards and the principles of interpretation that it employs must depend on whether or not divine initiative lies behind the human venture, whether or not the cultural process is a response to a divine imperative. But in the one context in which Christians have always spoken of such divine initiative, Tillich is unable to use this language at all.

A REINTERPRETATION OF CREATION

When Tillich discusses the doctrine of creation in his *Systematic Theology,* he offers an analysis of the creatureliness of all things for the traditional account of divine sovereignty and love. Protestantism is not obliged to interpret creation as an event that took place " once upon a time." [40] Instead, its real task is to discuss " the creatureliness of all things and their relation to the creative ground. The religious-mythical term ' creation ' must be interpreted by the religious-empirical term ' creaturely.' " [41] The myth of creation *ex nihilo,* though it is the basic description of the relation between God and the world, means only that creaturely being is essentially good but contingent. It signifies that finitude is not in itself tragic: " the tragic character of existence is not rooted in the creative ground of being; consequently, it does not belong to the essential nature of things." [42] It also points toward the element of nonbeing inherent in creatureliness which renders tragedy always possible and death a natural necessity.

But if these affirmations exhaust the meaning of the Biblical account of creation, what can be said of the divine attributes usually discussed in relation to the work of God as Creator?

Nothing at all can be said of the motivation for divine creativity — indeed, the question is not really admissible.

The divine life is creative, actualizing itself in inexhaustible abundance. The divine life and the divine creativity are not different. God is creative because He is God. Therefore, it is meaningless to ask whether creation is a necessary or a contingent act. [43]

As for divine transcendence, it is man's liberty to act against his essential unity with God that makes God transcendent to the world. " The divine transcendence is identical with the freedom of the created to turn away from the essential unity with the creative ground of its being." [44] But if the recognition of finite freedom is the one avenue that leads to the affirmation of divine transcendence, it certainly does not lead to more than a privative definition of it.

The meaning of the freedom of God is that what elicits our ultimate concern " is in no way dependent on man or on any finite being or on any finite concern." [45] God is free from his creatures, but is he also free for them? Is he at liberty to be with them and to shape the course of their history? When Tillich writes that God is " free to stand for the world," this is an ontological affirmation which simply means that if the finite did not participate in the power of being, it would not be at all. If finite freedom to fall from unity with its ground is in fact " identical with " divine transcendence, faith in a Lord active in the historical process, a God who has willed the existence of what is other than himself and willed to have commerce with it, is an illusion.

Tillich's existential reinterpretation of creation constantly emphasizes the inclusiveness of Being. Despite its rich diversification, Being is one. In *The Interpretation of History,* he wrote:

That every being participates in absolute being shows the seriousness of things. No being has unconditioned power of being, but each points through positive and negative qualities to the absolute power of being which it shares. . . . To see things in this transcendent quality is the presupposition of religious ontology; or, in dogmatic terminology, of the doctrine of creation, which, indeed, has lost more and more of the consciousness of its genuine meaning and has become the empty assertion that " God has created the world." [46]

But to say that God has created the world is not an " empty assertion " for the theology of culture. It affirms that the distinction between God and the world reflects the will of the Creator. It is not something to be overcome. It exists for the sake of the fulfillment of the creature. Tillich, however, stresses the ontological rather than the personal and ethical aspects of fallenness and redemption, which he defines as the reunion of the separated. He insists upon "the point of coincidence between the end of creation and the beginning of the Fall."

Fully developed creatureliness is fallen creatureliness. . . . To be outside the divine life means to stand in actualized freedom, in an existence which is no longer united with essence. Seen from one side, this is the end of creation. Seen from the other side, it is the beginning of the fall. . . . Creation is fulfilled in the creaturely self-realization which simultaneously is freedom and destiny. But it is fulfilled through separation from the creative ground through a break between existence and essence. Creaturely freedom is the point at which creation and fall coincide. This is the background of what is called "human creativity." [47]

Tillich never identifies finitude and fallenness, but his distinction between existence and estranged existence is very tenuous: "Actualized creation and estranged existence are identical." [48] Divine omnipotence means that "God is the power of being in everything that is, transcending every special power infinitely but acting at the same time as its creative ground." [49] Nevertheless, it is man himself who "is responsible for the transition from essence to existence because he has finite freedom." [50] Essence is that from which existence is fallen. Existence is fallen because it is the "actualization" of essence. The contrast between what man is and what he was created to be is radically subordinated to the contrast between existence and what "preceded" existence. [51] In his discussion of creation no less than in the context of Christology, Tillich obscures the question of divine volition and intent.

He cannot offer an unambiguous affirmation of finite existence because he cannot affirm that its source lies in a free and deliberate divine decision, in an " act of God."

The Christian tradition has attempted to balance two affirmations. To exist is to be estranged. To exist is also and first of all to be called by God to fulfill existence. In what Tillich has written, the focus lies mainly on the former. This existential interpretation of the Genesis story offers nothing to supplement what the symbol of the cross provides for the theology of culture. It renders it impossible to justify human creativity except insofar as " the ultimate meaning of existence shines through all finite forms of thought and action." [52] So every aspect of the human venture must be appraised in the light of its transparency, its capacity to point beyond itself to its ground. The meaning of this standard, finally, is that to exist is to be called not to fulfill existence but to bear witness to that unity of Being from which existence has fallen away.

In his interpretation of history, Tillich relies on three concepts which express different answers to the question of the *nomos* or law of life — autonomy, heteronomy, and theonomy. An autonomous culture means

the attempt to create the forms of personal and social life without any reference to something ultimate and unconditional, following only the demands of theoretical and practical rationality. A heteronomous culture . . . subjects the forms and laws of thinking and acting to authoritative criteria . . . even at the price of destroying the structures of rationality. A theonomous culture expresses in its creations an ultimate concern and a transcending meaning not as something strange but as its own spiritual ground.[53]

Heteronomy means imperialism, an imposition of alien standards on some dimension of life which violates its integrity.

A heteronomous situation always provokes a reaction in the name of autonomy. On the other hand, the relation between autonomy and theonomy is not entirely negative. Tillich says that the latter does not deny what is legitimate in autonomous aspirations. They are fulfilled and transcended by the theonomous recognition of the unconditional element that meaningful activity presupposes but does not itself ever possess. Autonomous cultural forms are filled with the contents of the holy, and the holy finds adequate expression in and through these profane forms.[54]

In fact, however, the relation between them does become purely negative. Autonomous form exists only in order to be overcome and rendered wholly transparent, no longer a thing in itself but only a medium through which " another thing which is beyond all things " is manifest.[55] Theonomy involves a blurring of the particularity of the various aspects of the cultural enterprise within an inclusive religious continuum, an obscuring of their integrity and relative independence. And in the historical writings of Tillich, autonomy and theonomy are always antithetical. He finds a recurrent pattern in history: no realization of theonomy is more than fragmentary, and every theonomous culture carries the seeds of its dissolution within itself as hidden aspirations toward autonomy. As the disintegrative effects of these trends become apparent, a heteronomous reaction appears in the form of a religious protest against emergent secularism. But theonomy cannot be restored. It is a matter of historical destiny, not of individual or corporate action. Nor can an autonomous culture long sustain itself:

Autonomy is able to live as long as it can draw from the religious tradition of the past, from the remnants of a lost theonomy. But more and more it loses this spiritual foundation. It becomes emptier, more formalistic, or more factual and is driven toward skepticism and cynicism, toward the loss of meaning and purpose.[56]

Sometimes it is dissolved in theonomy. Sometimes it plunges to bankruptcy. Always it is an irremediably unstable situation. Despite the frequency with which the word appears in the essays of Tillich, autonomy has little positive significance for his thought. Whether an instance of catastrophic pride or a penultimate stage in the progress of the finite toward renewed transparency to its ground and judge, autonomy is no more than a transitional moment within a larger historical dialectic.

Theonomy, transparency, the Protestant Principle, the existential reinterpretation of the doctrine of creation, the rejection of Biblical personalism because it renders the relations between God and the world external and transitory and subjects God to the polarities of finitude — all these confirm the suspicion that, for Tillich, the value of the finite does not reside in its integrity as the creation of God, willed and sustained by a free and sovereign Lord. Instead, its value lies in its potential holiness, since all things can become media for the manifestation of what is truly ultimate.

Tillich has radically conceived what it means to rely on the symbol of the cross to appraise the human venture. The themes of alienation, judgment, and redemption are extracted from the context which the Bible provides for them in the first chapters of Genesis. The factors that have inspired the distinctive option that Tillich espouses are less important than the option itself. Tillich has placed the cross at the center of the theology of culture. Part of the challenge of his achievement is that it raises the question of the limits of this approach.

The Christian vision contains a motif that is not expressed by the stark alternatives that Tillich envisions, either demonic pride or theonomy. It has affirmed that God freely willed the existence of that which is other than himself. He maintains it in its very distinction from himself for the sake of its own creaturely fulfillment. Man has been given his own particular vocation, for God is not jealous of what He has made. Most simply, the revelation of divine will and purpose and love in the cross of Christ has compelled Christians to contemplate the will and purpose and love involved in creation as well, because it is the Author of nature who has come to redeem man in Jesus of Nazareth. This affords a perspective much different from that of Tillich. But he has phrased the fundamental alternatives with boldness and clarity; his reliance on the cross captures the traditional emphasis of Protestantism. How much light does it cast on the artist's venture? How much justice can be done to the creative enterprise?

ART AND THE THEOLOGY OF CULTURE

Tillich understands the theology of culture as an attempt to penetrate to the

unconscious, self-evident faith which lies at a deeper level than the apparent antithesis of the belief and unbelief which both arise out of it and are both equally rooted in it. This unconscious faith which is not assailed because it is the presupposition of life and is lived rather than thought of, this all-determining, final source of meaning constitutes the actual religious situation.[57]

How is it possible to fathom those pervasive but unconscious assumptions about human nature and destiny which are the matrix for every expression of belief or unbelief? His answer is that they are revealed by the prevailing *style* of thought and action. He distinguishes between the form, content, and

import of human creativity.[58] The import or religious significance of a work of art is disclosed in and through its style.
It is because of its form that a work of art exists, and because
of its style that it shares something with contemporaneous
works. Every age and culture possesses its own particular
style, expressed " in its choice of objects, in the attitudes of its
creative personalities, in its institutions and customs." [59]

So style discloses a characteristic temper, not the product
of reflection but the basis for it, which implies some answer
to the question of the meaning of life. It is manifest most
vividly in the arts, which are the principal means for the
discovery of the actual religious situation.

If you want to know what is the ultimate self-interpretation of an
historical period, you must ask, " What kind of style is present in
the artistic creations of this period." Style is the over-all form
which, in the particular forms of every particular artist and of
every particular school, is still visible as the over-all form. . . .
The expression of that which unconsciously is present in this
period as its self-interpretation, as the answer to the question of
the ultimate meaning of its existence.[60]

For Tillich, statements about style are not simply empirical
generalizations. The import of human creativity is elusive.
" It is an art as much as a science to ' read styles,' and it requires religious intuition . . . to penetrate to the level where
an ultimate concern exercises its driving power." [61]

Tillich does not award any particular theological significance to the content of art. His definition of religion as ultimate concern, no matter how secular the fashion in which
the concern is expressed, and his description of religious symbolism in terms of transparency to the ground of being, mean
that the question of content is irrelevant. The standard by
which aesthetic images are judged is their ability to point

beyond their own form and content, not toward anything within the realm of existence but toward the inexhaustible power of being that animates all things.[62]

The Varieties of Style and Their Religious Meaning. In the course of time, new styles evolve and old ones disappear. But there are constant factors combined in one way or another in all of them. There are subjective elements, because of the imaginative powers the artist brings to his material. There are objective or realistic ones, because he incorporates into his work what he meets in our common world. There are idealistic elements, for art is always a transformation of reality. Every style has many ingredients. It is the manner in which they are related that affords the key for the appraisal of the religious situation.[63] What combination is the dominant motif at a particular time?

Tillich describes five possible types, all of which express man's relation to ultimate reality.[64] Each is related to a particular form of religious experience, but all reflect the ontological awareness of the unconditional. The first is sacramental, a numinous realism that "depicts ordinary things, ordinary persons, ordinary events . . . in a way which makes them strange, mysterious, laden with an ambiguous power." [65] This is characteristic of primitive art, which portrays ultimate reality as the power animating common objects. It is apparent in the development toward cubism from Cézanne to Braque, for this was an attempt to capture the "cosmic significance" of things. There is a certain mysticism in this sacramental approach, but mysticism tends to issue in a second type of style which dissolves what is finite and definite into a visual continuum. This was one aspect of impressionism. It is more apparent in nonobjective art, where

one can use basic structural elements of reality like lines, cubes, planes, colors, as symbols for that which transcends all reality. . . .

American artists have deprived reality of its manifoldness, of the concreteness of things and persons, and have expressed ultimate reality through the medium of elements which ordinarily appear only in unity with concrete objects.[66]

The third type is critical realism, the correlate of prophetic or protestant religion. To illustrate this style, he invokes Bosch, Bruegel, Goya, and Daumier. Their world has lost the numinous quality it possessed for sacramental realism, yet the inexhaustible richness in their " sober, objective, quasi-scientifically observed reality is a manifestation of ultimate reality, although it is lacking in directly numinous character." [67] Another style is idealism, of which Tillich is particularly skeptical because it habitually degenerates to superficial sentimentality. Even so, it has religious import, for it portrays man and his world in their essential and unfallen perfection and captures " the highest possibilities of being." [68] Finally, there is expressionism. Tillich uses the word to describe the combination of various stylistic elements in a distinctive vision. In this sense, it is a synonym for the individuality or imaginative power of the artist. But when expressionistic elements dominate a work of art, it is endowed with unique religious significance. Tillich argues that " while the others are only indirectly representing the ultimate, the expressive element represents it directly. . . . In itself it is essentially adequate to express religious meaning." [69] Only an expressionistic style is able to convey the character of ultimate reality as both the ground and the judge or abyss of the finite. Despite their implicit religious significance, no other style is directly faithful to both aspects of the unconditional. Expressionism captures the contingent and self-transcendent nature of the world

by using elements of it in a way which does not exist in the ordinarily encountered reality. Expressionism disrupts the naturally given appearance of things. Certainly, they are united in the artistic form, but not in a way which the imitating or the idealistic or even the realistic element would demand. On the other hand, that which is expressed is not the subjectivity of the artist in the sense of the subjective element which is predominant in Impressionism and Romanticism. That which is expressed is the " dimension of depth " in the encountered reality, the ground and abyss in which everything is rooted.[70]

Expressionism as a style is the correlate of belief-ful realism as an attitude, self-transcendent naturalism as an ontology, the Protestant Principle as a religious conviction. It is the aesthetic approximation of transparency. Whether or not it uses traditional religious imagery, it always has direct religious reference. Tillich has consistently adopted an affirmative stance toward modern art. Despite its portrayals of negation and meaninglessness, contemporary art remains an affirmation of the human condition, for " he who can bear and express meaninglessness shows that he experiences meaning within his desert of meaninglessness." [71] Several times Tillich has cited Picasso's *Guernica* as the greatest Protestant painting of our time — not because of any answer it offers, but because of the passionate way the question of ultimate meaning is raised by the artist's expressionistic style. In *Guernica,*

the " piece " character of our reality is perhaps more horribly visible than in any other of the modern pictures. . . . And if Protestantism means that, first of all, we do not have to cover up anything, but have to look at the human situation in its depths of estrangement and despair, then this is one of the most powerful religious pictures. And, although it has no religious content, it does have religious style in a very deep and profound sense.[72]

Levels of the Relation Between Religion and Art. Tillich describes four possible relationships between religion and art. The first involves nonreligious content and nonreligious style, by which he means one that is not primarily expressionistic. Yet every style has an implicit religious reference. An article of Protestant faith is that God is present in the secular no less than in the sacred. Even paintings like those of Steen and Rubens, in their vital affirmation of life, point indirectly toward the inexhaustible power that sustains contingent being. Second, there is the union of nonreligious content and religious style — expressionism. Art like that of De Chirico and Chagall expresses the disruption and estrangement of the modern world. They sought " to look into the depths of reality, below any surface and any beautification of the surface and any organic unity." [73] In this movement away from the surfaces of things toward planes and cubes, Tillich discerns a quest for ultimate meaning. It seems to him the most profound religious affirmation possible in the present age. Expressionism is a protest against " self-complacent finitude " in the name of what is truly ultimate, even though it sometimes tends to see the unconditional only as judge and abyss.

The third level is " dangerously irreligious," for it combines a nonreligious style with content that is " religious " in some traditional sense. But for two centuries men in the Western world have experienced " the disintegration of the symbols of ultimate concern in their particular religious tradition." [74] By definition, a style united with these now broken symbols cannot be more than conventional and academic. It is nonreligious because it is meretricious as a style. In every age, the attempt to portray religious subjects through a style not radically expressionistic has tended to degenerate to " idealized naturalism." But now it involves a real distortion and suppression of the truth, an " unwillingness to see and to face our real situation." [75] An attempt to return to what is an irrecoverable tradition, it is devoid of real creativity or expressiveness.

Finally, there is the possibility that expressionistic style and authentic religious content can be united. El Greco attained it in some of his paintings of the crucifixion theme and Mathias Grünewald in the Christ of the Isenheim altar. But Tillich is convinced that in the modern world, traditional religious symbols have been so fractured and eroded of their significance that this fourth level is no real option. Instead, the Christian must learn to appreciate the first two levels, even though their content is ostensibly nonreligious, and struggle to expose the vacuity of the third.

Despite his elaborate analysis of the arts, Tillich's conclusions are few. The religious quality of art does not depend on its content, for no authentic style is profane. All styles indirectly point toward what is ultimate. Expressionism has a direct religious reference, because its transformation of the surfaces of things affirms the self-transcendent character of reality and protests against the pretensions of the finite to be ultimate. " Ultimately," he claims, " no irreligious art is possible." [76] It is important to recognize that this is not a conclusion at which he arrives but the axiom with which he begins, the assumption on which his whole venture is predicated. He writes of the arts only to illustrate within a particular sphere the validity of a thesis universally applicable: that religion is the substance of culture, culture the form of religion.

Man's experience and his world everywhere point beyond themselves toward a ground of being and meaning. Were the finite not to participate in this unconditioned reality, it would not be. Art, like all else, indirectly conveys the self-transcendent character of the world. It can do no less. The presupposition of all cultural activity is an obscure recognition of something unconditional, some knot that anchors the thread from which the fabric of meaningful existence is woven. Tillich's analysis of styles is intended to show the various ways this religious awareness manifests itself in the artist's venture, just as it does in every other serious cultural activity. It is also possible to speak of levels of the relation between religion and art, for the ideal style is one that directly conveys the import of man's ontological certainty. Expressionism accomplishes this, because its disclosure of the contingent and relative nature of all things is an explicit witness to the ultimacy of what is truly ultimate.

Certainly Tillich has carried a gospel to the cultured despisers. Despite man's indifference and hostility toward religion, there remains a religious dimension to all life. But if all art is religious, what is religious art? If everything is religious, then what is religious at all? The only question for the theology of art finally is this: does the artist attempt to disguise the contingency and self-transcendent character of things, to which his work nonetheless remains at least indirect witness? This question is the subject of Tillich's explorations in the history of art.

Art and the Interpretation of History. In a remarkable essay titled "The World Situation," Tillich argues that it is possible to trace the rise and decline of bourgeois society through the art of the painter. The ontological awareness involved in all creativity assumes an increasingly idolatrous form and eventually generates a reaction against itself. The first phase of the life of the bourgeoisie was its revolutionary struggle against a disintegrating feudal culture. Then came the triumph of the new society, the creation of a world mechanism of production and exchange. Finally the day of reckoning arrived, as modern industrial culture reduced men to the status of things, subjects to objects, ends to means, in a process without ultimate goal. Art influenced by the spirit of capitalism was an expression of complacent finitude and a disclosure of spiritual exhaustion. To illustrate these phases, Tillich cites Giotto, Titian, Rembrandt, and Sargent.

Giotto's portraits of Francis of Assisi and his followers convey a sense of the divine power " by which man is possessed and elevated beyond his individual character and personal experiences." [77] They tell of the capacity of all finite being to point beyond itself. In Titian this sense of a transcendent power is gone. He celebrates the beauty and power of man. For Giotto, it was faith in the transcendent that invested life with meaning. For Titian, it was belief in the divinity of man and the humanity of the divine. The focus of Rembrandt's work lies in the tragedy and challenge of individual life. He was concerned with the unique individual, and not, like Titian, with the individual simply as the exemplar of the universal attributes of humanity. The art of Titian discloses a radically changed cultural situation: meaning has its source in what is immanent, not transcendent. The art of Rembrandt reflects another change: meaning has its source in what is individual, not universal. The subject of his portraits is

the personality of the early bourgeois spirit, still subject to absolute forces, still shaped by the Protestant conscience, but already standing by itself, independent alike of transcendent grace and of humanity. In these three painters the development of the ideal of personality in the modern world finds classic expression. If we take the long step to portraits painted since the middle of the nineteenth century, we are in still another world. Individuals with a highly developed intellectuality and strong will appear — the bearers of technical reason, the creators of large-scale world economy, of the great monopolies, the conquerors of the forces of nature and the anonymous directors of the world-wide mechanism of capitalistic society. Personality has become at once the ruler and the servant of Leviathan. Will-power and technical rationality are united, and thus the way is prepared for the Fascist type in which the last remnants of the classical and humanistic ideal of personality are completely lost.[78]

With the nineteenth century, the transition from medieval theonomy to autonomy was complete and the bankruptcy of autonomous pretensions became impossible to ignore. The triumphant bourgeoisie was " dominated by purposes without ultimate meaning and by sensations and actions without spiritual center." [79] Its art was pervaded by a complacent sense of self-sufficiency. Because it portrayed the world in a wholly mechanistic way, a naturalistic style accompanied the growth of industrial society. But naturalism also threatened the victory of bourgeois culture, for it disclosed the estrangement of man from man and of man from nature. So it was abandoned for a retreat to subjectivity.

Impressionism is subjective naturalism which uses objective reality with all of its distortions and horrors as material for aesthetic intuition. It is a method of escape, available only to those belonging directly or indirectly to the ruling groups.[80]

In its subjective form as impressionism, in its objective form as realism, naturalistic style prevailed throughout the century.[81] The cultural situation, degenerate autonomy, precluded the emergence of any other. Idealism was no more than an ideological maneuver on the part of the middle classes to cloak " the naturalistic face of Leviathan. When this veil was torn away by the contradictions of history and the rapid proletarianization of this group, they often became the principal supporters of Fascism." [82] But finally there appeared expressionist and surrealistic reactions against naturalism in art and its metaphysical implications. These were revolutionary movements protesting the dehumanization of man and the loss of the meaning of life. Painters like Cézanne and Van Gogh and Munch began to rediscover the depth of things, the dimensions beneath the surfaces with which impressionism and realism were concerned. And we who have encountered the demonic consequences of the aspiration to autonomy are their inheritors, yearning for the restoration of true theonomy.

A FOOTNOTE AGAINST RELIGION

Tillich's venture has a magisterial simplicity. Human activity is invested with significance because it always has an implicit religious dimension, and this furnishes the standard by which to appraise it. Is it transparent to that in which it must participate or else fall into meaninglessness and oblivion? The profane and secular must submit to the judgment of the holy and sacred element which alone sustains them. But there are problems that are not resolved by this simplicity. The idea of transparency conflicts with the way the creative enterprise originates in man's ambition to improve his commerce with the world. It has already been argued that aesthetic activity is inspired by the elemental necessity to carve up experience at its joints into determinate things and relationships. Its source lies in man's concern for the particularity and concreteness of the ingredients of experience. The artist's venture is elicited by man's relation to his environment and contributes in a fundamental way to its improvement.

Tillich appraises the creative enterprise in the light of its witness to the self-transcendent nature of reality rather than in the context of its disclosure of the specificity of things. From his perspective, concern with particularity for its own sake is an instance of blindness and pride — blindness because all finite things do point beyond themselves, pride because it implies the independence and self-sufficiency of what is contingent and relative. His standard also is at odds with what Huizinga calls the play element in the arts. Play means removal from ordinary life, the creation of a separate realm with severely defined limits. It means a game isolated from all else, pointing toward nothing. This spontaneous exercise of the free imagination, intent simply upon forms and colors that please the eye, neither knows nor seeks to know anythings that lies outside or beyond itself.

The tension between the idea of transparency and the utilitarian and playful aspects of the artist's venture is purely theoretical, however. It does not involve the imposition of alien standards upon the arts, for,

if the idea of God includes ultimate reality, everything that expresses ultimate reality expresses God whether it intends to do so or not. And there is nothing that could be excluded from this possibility because everything that has being is an expression, however preliminary and transitory it may be, of being-itself, of ultimate reality. . . . It is the riddle and the depth of all expression that it both reveals and hides at the same time. . . . There is ultimate reality in this stone and this tree and this man. They are translucent toward ultimate reality, but they are also opaque. They prevent it from shining through them. They try to exclude it. . . . In the same way, while trying to express reality in esthetic images, art makes ultimate reality manifest through these images — the word image, taken in its largest sense, which includes lingual and musical figures.[83]

But if the conflict is only theoretical, that does not lessen its importance. Tillich's standard obscures rather than clarifies the reasons why the artist's venture is important and what functions it performs within the cultural process. Tillich answers the question of the importance of the arts by describing their capacity to point toward that from which life has fallen away. This is a potential that art shares with all other forms of activity; its powers of transparency do not differentiate it from anything else. Tillich manages to offer both too little and too much: art is swallowed up in an omnivorous religious continuum, but shorn of its distinctive characteristics, evaluated in the light of a norm that contradicts its principal functions.

Tillich believes that the arts are important for Christian thought because the prevailing aesthetic style "always furnishes the most sensitive barometer of a spiritual climate." [84] But it is very difficult to accept such a claim. As he views the matter, whether nineteenth-century painting expressed or protested against the spirit of capitalism, it was ultimately shaped by socioeconomic forces. In fact, the relationships among painters are far more organic and complex than Tillich's reliance on contrasting "isms" would suggest. Cézanne was a pioneer, although perhaps not in the sense Tillich believes, but his painting also displays great continuity with that of his predecessors. He spoke of his own work as an attempt to unite the classical elements of Poussin with the immediacy and vividness of the impressionists, so that impressionism would become something "solid and durable." [85]

What is important is that the history of painting possesses continuity as well as a certain independence of other cultural developments because it is first of all an exploration of the distinctive technical problems involved in the use of some particular expressive media. A revival of interest in light and color inspired the impressionists to try to capture the instantaneity of the eye's response to the world. Goya and Velazquez contributed something to their awareness of how virtually inexhaustible were the possible variations of visual form. Can impressionism be interpreted from a theological perspective as a retreat to the subjective, inspired by the way that realism portrayed the estrangement of man from man and of man from nature in modern industrial society? The problem is not that Tillich is wrong so much as that he is irrelevant. His analysis does not touch the level on which the factors that really motivated impressionism operate. His judgments on the painting of the nineteenth century are evidence on behalf of Jacques Maritain's comment that

there is no more misleading and unsound literary genus than ideological systematization of human history intent on disregarding the essentials of art, and its intrinsic laws of development, for the sake of a so-called cultural diagnosis and prognosis of art as a moral symptom.[86]

Painting is so much a matter of the discovery of new resources in its own particular medium, and of advances in technique or new combinations of older ones, that it neither expresses so directly nor is determined so decisively by the contemporary spiritual climate as Tillich alleges. No fault can be found with his passion to overcome the separation of religion from culture that characterizes modern life. But he emphasizes the fundamental unity of life so much that the diversity of its various aspects is obscured, their independence of one another forgotten, their fidelity to their own laws of development ignored.

Behind Tillich's venture in the theology of culture lies a vision of the inclusiveness of Being which differs from that of the Bible, despite his reliance on the symbol of the cross. He rejects the Biblical story of creation as an act of God, a free and deliberate expression of divine love, because to him such language implies that God and the world somehow exist " beside " each other. He avoids the question of divine volition. For the myth of creation through the Word, and the externality of relationship it suggests, he substitutes the image of participation. And in this context, the only alternatives for the human venture are transparency to its ground or sterility and meaninglessness.

In the second century, Christianity confronted in Marcion its most dangerous adversary. His gospel of redemption, in certain ways so similar to the preaching of the Christian community, threatened the survival of the church more than any persecution. Against every form of gnosticism, the church kept faith with its monotheistic heritage by affirming the unity of Creator and Redeemer. Christians believe that the cross represents the supreme instance of deliberate divine initiative in the whole span of history. So they found themselves, in opposition to Marcion, also compelled to speak of creation in terms of divine initiative, decision, and love.

Christianity is distinguished from gnosticism by its claim that the cross points beyond itself toward another image, contained in the first chapters of Genesis. The cross alone does not furnish an adequate perspective for the interpretation of existence; the themes of estrangement and redemption must be supplemented by the myth of creation. Because He who came for man's redemption is the Creator of nature, the revelation at Calvary inspires faith that love also lies at the ultimate origin of things. In *The Protestant Era,* Tillich writes that when one is asked for proof of the fall of the world, the answer is,

a religious culture beside a secular culture, a temple beside a town hall, a Lord's Supper beside a daily supper, prayer beside work, meditation beside research, *caritas* beside *eros.*[87]

As the language of devotion, it is superb. As the expression of an ontological vision, it fails to do justice to God the Creator or to the freedom that he has awarded to what he has made.

Tillich's ambition to interpret the contemporary spiritual temper through its cultural expressions and to criticize them in the light of the Christian message has opened new and important areas for theological investigation. But the standard he employs conflicts with the real concern of the artist, and is at odds with the play element in his venture. It violates the certain independence of the artist's enterprise and fails to clarify the importance of what he does.

The particular merit of Tillich is that he has placed the cross at the heart of his interpretation of the human enterprise. But the cross cannot stand alone. To exist means to be fallen, and Christians are called to bear witness to that from which existence has fallen. But to exist also means to be called by God to the fulfillment of existence. For the Christian community, the images of creation and cross are inseparably bound up with each other. Each offers a perspective that corrects and amplifies the other. Tillich's reliance on the cross alone is faithful neither to the full resources of the Christian vision nor to the actualities of the artist's venture.

The cross points beyond itself.

III

NICOLAS BERDYAEV AND THE IMAGE OF CONSUMMATION

THE POINT OF VIEW

Man's freedom and his true vocation as creativity: these refrains inform all that Nicolas Berdyaev ever wrote. Disavowing ontological speculation and every form of dogmatism, he wanted men to recognize the reality and rich possibilities of their freedom. In an age that witnessed new and terrible varieties of tyranny, Berdyaev never ceased to protest against every betrayal of liberty. He had genius for investing traditional religious symbols with some novel significance, and he used all his talent to freight the imagery of the Christian story with a distinctive vision that is one enduring option for a theology of culture.

Berdyaev was convinced that his own Christian personalism was a radical departure from the Western philosophical tradition, which he believed had never affirmed man's liberty. In *Solitude and Society,* he wrote that his concern was not ontology but freedom, not the world but man, not objects but subjects, not nature but spirit, not contemplation and intellect, but will, action, creativeness.[1] Freedom and spirit are the proper stuff of philosophy: " Spirit is not an epiphenomenon of the material world, the material world is an epiphenomenon of spirit." [2] Investigations of the nature of things simply mean surrender without protest to the tyranny the world exerts over man. Freedom, not being, is primordial and the "absolute principle."[3] So the only serious philosophical question is the question of man.

But if men are free, their freedom is dreadful: they can choose bondage instead of liberty. Personality means the limitless capacity for self-transcendence. If a person does not orient himself toward the infinite and eternal, he becomes the victim of the finite and temporal. He is not self-sufficient. He requires an other. Freedom is found when he turns toward the realm of the spirit. He becomes a slave when he turns toward things, the domain of necessity.[4] But all men fall from freedom, betrayed into bondage by their will to power. Berdyaev's word for inauthentic existence is objectification, which means that men's actions are determined by factors outside themselves.

They submit to the tyranny of the impersonal and general. They accept the authority of " they say," even though who " they " are can never be specified. They create idols which serve the will to power because they are " mine but not yours " — class, race, nation, family. And then on the altars of these false gods they sacrifice their liberty.[5] But it is not only the will to power that condemns man to inauthentic existence. The subject-object structure of consciousness confirms the reign of the idols. It divides rather than unites. It seems both a cause and consequence of man's fall. Authentic knowledge means participation and communion in which the distinction between subject and object is overcome.[6]

Berdyaev uses objectification to designate the way the world is, as well as man's inauthentic ways of knowing and acting in the world. It is the fallen nature of the universe itself which lures man to the betrayal of his freedom.

Objectivization has two aspects: on the one hand it denotes the fallen, divided and servile world, in which the existential subjects, the personalities, are materialized. On the other hand, it comprehends the agency of the personal subject, of spirit, tending to reinforce ties and communications in this fallen world.[7]

His meaning is not simply that the ways in which persons are reduced to things in our society reinforce each individual's tendency to exploit his neighbors. For Berdyaev, the fallenness of the world is far more radically conceived.

Can it be maintained that objective knowledge is in itself deficient and sinful? . . . *The state of sin, of deficiency and degradation, should be attributed to Being rather than to knowledge.* In its degraded state knowledge can only apprehend an already degraded Being.[8]

Does this imply that the whole realm of the visible and tangible has emerged through some cosmic fall? Does it mean the rejection of the Biblical affirmation that " God saw everything that he had made, and behold, it was very good " (Gen. 1:31)? Berdyaev offers his own alternative to the Genesis story.

THE MYTH OF THE *UNGRUND*

Berdyaev's vision is rooted in a mythology of freedom that resembles some currents in medieval mysticism, especially the speculations of Eckhart and Boehme concerning the *Gottheit* or *Ungrund*. Boehme used the image to describe the mysterious depths and dynamism of the divine nature. Berdyaev, however, uses it to designate a reality "beside" God, a primordial realm of pure potentiality, eternal possibilities for both good and evil. The myth transforms the Genesis account of creation into the story of a demiurge forever struggling with what lies outside himself. But it expresses in a single metaphor the primacy of freedom over being, dynamics rather than form, will instead of intellect, mystery not *logos,* tragedy and creativity rather than " world harmony."

The contradictory, suffering, and flamingly tragic character of the life of the world is accounted for by the fact that before being and deeper than being lies the *Ungrund,* the bottomless abyss, irrational mystery, primordial freedom, which is not derivable from being . . . bottomless, indeterminate will. But this is a nothingness which is *Ein Hunger zum Etwas.* . . . In the darkness of the *Ungrund* a fire flames up and this is freedom, meonic, potential freedom. . . . Will, that is, freedom, is the beginning of everything.[9]

Freedom is no less ultimate than God. Its source lies in the darkness of the *Ungrund.* Man's liberty cannot be called the gift of the Creator. Like divine freedom, it evolves from the *Ungrund;* its powers for creation and destruction are neither controlled nor wholly known by God. He calls man to engage in the transfiguration of the tragic potentialities of this primordial freedom and in the creation of the greatest possible meaning and value. But he cannot coerce. Man is his partner, not his pawn.

The myth served Berdyaev in several ways — first, because it stresses the reality of the dialogue between God and man. If freedom is simply one attribute that the Creator has awarded the creature, if all its potentialities are comprehended within the eternal divine vision, then it seemed to Berdyaev there could be no genuine dialogue at all. God would converse with himself through his creatures, but he would not really converse with them.[10] If history means anything, man as well as God must possess freedom primordial and underived. In this respect, divine and human freedom are no different. So the myth also expresses the conviction that man can create new meanings and values that would remain unactualized forever, were it not for human agency. God himself could not realize them, for their source is man's heritage from what is outside the divine life. The course of human history is not " unnecessary, insignificant, having no relation to the inner life of the Deity and therefore, in the last resort, meaningless." [11] If it were, Berdyaev believed, the mystery of suffering could never be resolved; man would have no choice but to rebel against God.

Nothing shaped his theology more profoundly than Ivan's meditation on world harmony and children's tears in *The Brothers Karamazov*.[12] In his book on Dostoevsky he wrote:

> If freedom does not exist as a mystery behind all creation then we can admit neither the verity of this suffering world nor of a God who could create so horrible and meaningless a thing. . . . To be able to understand this world, to keep one's faith in its deep meaning, to reconcile the existence of God with the existence of evil it is absolutely necessary that each one of us should have this irrational freedom in him.[13]

Critics of Berdyaev argue that the myth contributes little toward the justification of God's way to man, for when God created human souls in eternity he knew of the tragic possibilities that would be involved in man's freedom. But that liberty also means powers to create what otherwise could never be achieved, powers that invest human history with far greater import than it has seemed to possess for traditional theism. Suffering does not reflect the will of God, but he cannot overcome it alone. He appeals to man for aid in the transformation of the dark potentialities of the *Ungrund*.

This mythology is the core of what Berdyaev called " esoteric Christianity." He offered it as an alternative to traditional patterns of thought which stress obedience, humility, the sovereignty of God, and a forensic understanding of redemption. It was especially the Old Testament witness to divine power and transcendence that Berdyaev opposed, calling it the product of a slave mentality.

The Hebrew mind, suppressed and frightened, knows God as a terrible commander, an autocratic master. Such a conception of God is incompatible with Christianity as a religion of divine-humanity. There can be no intimate relationship with a God who is a terrible commander, an autocratic master.[14]

According to Berdyaev it is God's refusal to exercise power which is the gauge of his love. He expresses his divinity precisely in his determination to conserve the reality of freedom and overcome every variety of slavery and constraint.[15] God actually has " less power than a policeman." [16] The idea of causality is wholly inapplicable to his relation to man and the world. The realm of time and space is ruled by " the prince of this world." In it God suffers, he does not govern.[17]

Berdyaev writes of the preexistence of the human soul; it belongs to the eternal, not the temporal. Human freedom evolves from the *Ungrund*. What is there in the world of time and space that God has made? Berdyaev answers, " We reject the view, widespread in theological teaching, that God is the cause of the world." [18] On the first page of his autobiography, he declared:

I cannot remember my first cry on encountering the world, but I know for certain that from the very beginning I was aware of having fallen into an alien realm. . . . I have always been a pilgrim. Christians ought to feel that they have no abiding city on earth, and they should be seekers of the city to come. . . . The consciousness of being rooted in the earth was alien to me, and I was strongly attracted to the Orphic myth concerning the origin of the human soul, which speaks of a falling away of man's spirit from a higher world into a lower.[19]

Many times he acknowledged his debt to Schopenhauer, who confirmed his " sense of the unallayed pain of human existence." [20] He called himself a Christian gnostic and spoke of his liking for Marcion. [21] Both of them, acutely sensitive to the mystery of suffering, wanted to exonerate God from all blame for the creation of a world brutal and absurd. [22] Both followed the same road to achieve it: the divorce of power from love, creation from redemption, Old Testament from New.

His description of inauthentic existence as objectification and the way he relates the subject-object structure of consciousness to man's fall convey Berdyaev's stance toward the world. It is not a home but a prison. Salvation means release from its torment. [23] As he interprets Christian faith, it becomes the apotheosis of creativity, coupled with a radical denial of the world itself. His God is creative, constantly at work to redeem a fallen universe from objectification, but Creator of heaven and earth He is not.

When art and the human venture are interpreted in the context of a vision such as this, several questions are difficult to resolve. The first concerns man the rebel. The problem does not arise from the way aesthetic activity is related to eschatology, but from the way consummation is divorced from creation, eschatology from the Genesis story. Since God is not responsible for this world, consummation does not mean the fulfillment of history and creaturely life as we know it now, but release from the world's tyranny. The creative exercise of freedom which is man's proper vocation is in no way a response to the world. It is the attempt to transfigure what in itself seems bereft of meaning and beauty. The artist's venture is not an affirmation but a repudiation of things, a disclosure of man's passion to escape everything definite and circumscribed. It is not inspired by what the Creator has done, but is a participation in God's own struggle to redeem the objectification of primordial freedom. Yet is the artist so much a rebel? Is his venture elicited only by what the world lacks, not at all by what the world has?

A second question concerns human freedom. Man belongs to the processes of nature which he also transcends. He is not only spirit but incarnate spirit. The ironic consequence of Berdyaev's reluctance to accept both aspects of man's nature is that freedom itself becomes problematical. Berdyaev is not able to affirm the field or context which is necessary for the exercise of any liberty at all that is distinctively finite and human. In the name of freedom he protests against all that confines and limits man. Yet when all constraint is gone, human freedom has disappeared as well. It has lost the structure that provides it with determinate possibilities to actualize. The freedom of which Berdyaev writes is born in the moment all limits are transcended. But is this not also the moment of its death? These limits are what endow freedom with concrete potentialities.

Berdyaev possessed a tragic vision, for he recognized that men were free to disavow their freedom. It is a tragic vision because for him Christianity meant "a revelation of a Kingdom which is not of this world and which signifies that there is no making out anything in this world." [24] It is tragic because existence does not allow the exercise of the kind of freedom for which Berdyaev hungered. Men can achieve it only in "symbolic" fashion. And even that would be impossible, were it not for the Christ.

CHRIST THE LIBERATOR

Berdyaev tells us that the work of Christ is misunderstood when it is phrased in terms of justification, atonement, and reconciliation. This forensic language establishes a scheme in which divine sovereignty and human impotence are juxtaposed. But the relation between God and man is a mystery of freedom, not power. The cross is not the revelation of divine judgment upon human pretension; it is a symbol of the compassion of God for the tragic human condition.[25] The plight of man is not that he is a rebel but a slave, bound to the world of things.[26] Christ comes to liberate men from captivity and restore the freedom they have betrayed and lost in the fallen world. He

exorcises the spell and casts off the fetters of necessity. He is the Liberator. *Without Christ the Liberator, the world would have remained for all time shattered in necessity and determinism would be for ever true.*[27]

Berdyaev writes of two forms of freedom, the irrational freedom to choose either good or evil and the greater liberty into which men are ushered through the choice of the good — what Augustine called man's *libertas maior*. Christ restores to men the original freedom of Adam which degenerated into compulsion and constraint when it was exercised for evil instead of good.[28] Berdyaev insisted that the divine-human relation is distorted if Christ is understood to convey man's *libertas maior* apart from the restoration of his original freedom of choice. To be human is to be free: what is good for man not only must confer freedom upon him, it must be freely chosen by him. In *Freedom and the Spirit* he wrote:

Let us face the fact that true freedom is only possible in and through Christ, that Christ, whatever may be said, must be freely accepted and that it is by a free spiritual act that we must come to him. . . . Freedom cannot be the result of constraint even were this constraint divine. . . . Human freedom is not only freedom in God, but also freedom in relation to God. Man must be free in respect of God, the world, and his own nature.[29]

Berdyaev wanted an interpretation of history that would not allow it to end where it began, merely with the restoration of man to the status he enjoyed before the Fall. He argued that redemption is not the goal but only a penultimate stage in the drama of God and man. Christ comes to restore man's original freedom so that he can attain a greater one. This *libertas maior* is not simply the freedom that accompanies loyalty to what is good, but the freedom to create the good. Man is redeemed for a higher life, creativity. Berdyaev never wavered from his conviction that

man's life could not be created by God only for the purpose that having sinned he should atone for his sin, and should put into the work of his redemption all his powers, throughout the whole extent of the world process. Such a conception of human nature . . . would demean the God-like dignity of man. The absolute Christian truth turns on the one hand toward redemption from sin and evil and on the other towards the positive creative calling of man.[30]

He believed that traditional Christian thought had obscured the significance of man's liberty by its interpretation of the divine-human relation entirely in terms of pride and estrangement, judgment and redemption. Its vision of man's nature and destiny was simply an unconscious expression of our fallenness. So through the Christian era men have been lacerated by impossible alternatives, either man without God or God without man, human creation without Christianity or Christianity without creativity. The late Renaissance chose the former, the Middle Ages the latter, and the modern epoch reveals the bankruptcy of the options themselves.[31]

Berdyaev was convinced that Christ came to reveal the divinity of mankind. Apart from the Liberator, men know freedom only in the paradoxical form of necessity and bondage to the world of objects. He brings them liberty to choose what is truly good. But creativity would be only illusion if man did not possess a divine element in himself, the legacy of the *Ungrund*. To bring forth new meaning and value from this heritage is truly a divine activity, though not the prerogative of God alone.[32] These human labors contribute to the Kingdom of God. Perhaps there has been no more impassioned an avowal of synergism in the history of Christian thought than Berdyaev's words, " It is precisely the human independence of the divine, human freedom, and man's creative activity, which are divine." [33] And in *Freedom and the Spirit* these characteristic lines appear:

Man out of the depths of this freedom . . . continues the work of creation. Man is not a slave, still less a mere nothing, and he co-operates with the divine task of achieving a creative victory over nothingness. Man is necessary to God, and God suffers when man fails to be conscious of his own usefulness. God helps man, but man must also help God.[34]

But this final freedom of the children of God can be achieved in time and space only in a fractured way. Now creativity is fated to remain " symbolic," although in eternity it will be theurgy, full participation in God's own creativeness.

Berdyaev's gnostic vision influences his interpretation of the person and work of Christ, for he argues that history is not an appropriate medium for the revelation of God. Time is the consequence of man's fall from eternity. " The Fall could not have taken place in the natural world, because this world is itself the result of the Fall. The Fall . . . in fact, produced time." [35] But then what is the meaning of Bethlehem? Christ is the Liberator because through him men grasp the truth of the divinity of mankind. But is it Christ himself or the truth he represents which is important? The man or the myth? [36] In either event, for Berdyaev the redemptive work of Christ does not mean the advent of God in the realm of time and space, but the elevation of the finite into the infinite and the human into the divine. Its purpose is to turn inside out the enslaved consciousness of fallen man by the disclosure of his true divinity. But it is no longer a story of the humility and condescension of God, become bone of our bone and flesh of our flesh. It no longer inspires an affirmation of the world on the grounds that God himself has truly entered into it.

There are many criticisms that can be directed against Berdyaev. The least systematic and most metaphorical of writers, he believed truth lay as often with heretics such as Marcion as it did in orthodoxy. He did not hesitate to reject much of the Christian tradition. But if he is vulnerable to criticism, this must not obscure his real significance. No Christian interpretation of the human enterprise can afford to ignore his call for some greater recognition of the integrity and potential of man's freedom than the themes of estrangement and redemption alone imply. They must be supplemented in some way that will admit man's creative powers and prerogatives in this world. As he wrote in *The Destiny of Man:*

It is curious that theologians fail to recognize the presence of freedom in artistic creation, and only think of it with reference to the Fall, guilt and punishment. This is the weakness of theological theories which renders them unable to justify man's creative activity and provide a basis for it.[37]

Man has come to new maturity in the modern age, constrained to recognize new dimensions of his freedom and more of its vast potentialities for creation and destruction. Nicolas Berdyaev was a pioneer in the search for a new grammar and rhetoric that would ally faith and freedom.

THE TRAGEDY OF CULTURE

But if revelation through Christ frees men to realize the possibilities involved in their heritage of freedom, the fallen world still holds them in its bondage. Berdyaev phrases the tragic character of the human venture in several ways. In all activity there is a lacerating disparity between the creative impulse and its expression. There is an ineradicable antagonism between authentic creativity and the impulse to develop and conserve cultural values. And there is the tragic ambivalence of every symbol.

Creativity is eschatological. It is always an attempt to bring this world to its end. But as soon as the creative impulse is expressed, it is swallowed up within the sphere of objectification, within the domain of the subject-object structure of consciousness that marks our fallen condition. Every concrete expression of creativity, because it stands over against its author as an object, confirms the power the fallen world still exerts over man. So the real meaning of every work of art is that we are impotent to achieve the transfiguration of the objectified universe which the creative impulse intends.

The failure of the creative act consists in this, that it does not achieve its purpose of bringing this world to an end, of overcoming its objectivity. Its success, on the other hand, lies in the preparation it makes for the transformation of the world, for the Kingdom of God. . . . It follows, therefore, that the creative embodiments which man produces are two-fold in their nature, the conflict between the two worlds is, so to speak, reflected in them. But for all that, there is nothing more terrible, more hopeless, nothing more tragic than every act of realization.[88]

The artist's labors do not refine or augment his original creative intuition, they debase it. Expression means surrender to

the fallen structure of the world, the distortion and diminish-
ment of what is expressed. Creativity contributes everything
to art. Art contributes nothing to enrich and clarify the initial
creative vision.

It would be difficult to apply these comments to painting
or sculpture, however. As Collingwood says, a painter " paints
things because until he has painted them he doesn't know
what they are like." [39] He was not defending the theory of
art as imitation, but simply insisting that through the creation of art, men learn more about reality than they knew before. Only through some deliberate act of expression, whether
gesture or word or song, is awareness transformed into significant apprehension. Incarnation is not failure but fulfillment. A sculptor responds to the exigencies of the material
he has freely chosen, and the resources of that physical medium are partly what he is intent on celebrating. He is a man
who has a creative vision, but he is also someone with a great
passion for looking at and shaping wood or stone.

The other tragic aspects that Berdyaev sees in the human
venture are variations on this same theme. The creative impulse wants another world and is unconcerned to realize
possibilities in this one. Yet that is all it can achieve, cultural
values whose existence testifies to the frustration of its aim.
Creativeness is inimical to the conservation of all it can
produce. It seeks a new mode of existence where the subject-
object polarity will be overcome. It attains this only symbolically, in the realm of imagination but not in fact. It even-
tuates in books, paintings, and other artifacts which are all
ambivalent because they each add to the mass of the fallen
universe.

Convinced of the antagonism of authentic creativeness toward cultural activity, Berdyaev was haunted by the question
of nihilism. In *The Meaning of the Creative Act,* he wrote

most passionately of the lack of ultimate justification for the human enterprise.

In both its most profound essence and its religious meaning culture is a great failure. Philosophy and science are failures in the creative knowledge of truth; art and literature are failures in the creation of beauty; the family and sex life are failures in the creation of love; morals and law have failed in the creation of human relationships. . . . Culture has crystallized all man's failures. All the achievements of culture are symbolic rather than realistic. . . . Culture is eternally and tragically unsatisfied. . . . Culture's failure and dissatisfaction come from the fact that in everything culture achieves an evil endlessness but never reaches the eternal. Culture only creates an evil endlessness, an endless mediocrity. Hence culture, metaphysically speaking, is bourgeois.[40]

But he did not regard nihilism as legitimate. As the road from barbarism, the cultural process is a stage in man's progress toward freedom. Even though culture is the product of the distortion of the creative impulse, it provides men with a sort of tenuous community that is better than none.[41] And while it is a symbolic and not a real victory, at least it is a symbol and fractured prophecy of man's ultimate triumph over objectification. So the claims of the human venture have a certain legitimacy. Cultural activity retains a certain ambiguous value — not because of its own intrinsic meaning, but because of what it symbolizes; not because it is an expression of true creativeness, but because of what is distorted and diminished in this objectification; not because it leads necessarily to freedom, but because it is a victory over barbarism.[42]

But its dubious validity and the symbolic character of its values must never be forgotten. Berdyaev identifies the confusion of symbol and reality with the classical spirit. In his interpretation of history he constantly employs the contrast between classical and romantic. They describe conflicting visions of the world, one pagan and the other Christian.[43] The classical spirit affirms the finite in its finitude; it fears the infinite and is anti-eschatological. It means objectification,

the imprisonment of spirit in a finite and perfect form. The subjective becomes the objective, the infinite becomes the finite, and in these dead forms the creative fire is extinguished.[44]

The romantic passion for the infinite leaves it dissatisfied with all that is finite. It is eschatological, aware of the alien character of this earth. It knows the meaning of the finite does not lie in itself. Classicism accepts the subject-object duality of finite being and knowing as ultimate; romanticism denies it and aspires toward a form of communion with all life in which that polarity is overcome.[45]

Berdyaev distinguishes between culture and civilization in a way reminiscent of Spengler.[46] Both seek to transform the squalor of the world and free man from its tyranny. But civilization represents the final triumph of the classical temper. It emerges as skeptical rationalism erodes the myths by which culture lived and from which it derived an organic character. Civilization has no use for myth and symbol; it is the product of the will to power. Culture cannot achieve more than a symbolic transfiguration of the world. Men either forget its ambiguity and confuse symbol with reality, or else they eventually repudiate cultural ideals in the search for a way to effect a real transformation of things. So civilization is born from the failure of culture.[47]

Civilization means reliance upon technical advances alone for the transfiguration of life. It precipitates a profound alteration in man's relation to nature. But if he escapes from the sovereignty of the Great Pan, he becomes the captive of his own tools. The last form of bondage is worse than the first.[48] The real tragedy of civilization, however, is not that men are enslaved by means they have themselves created. The temptation to confuse symbol and reality that is involved in all cultural activity is now realized absolutely. Civilization is rooted in the repudiation of the principle of symbolism itself, as the nature of its antagonism toward culture reveals. Affirming its own ultimacy, it renders impossible any authentic creativity at all. The creation of men who believe themselves gods, its fate is bankruptcy, meaninglessness, bondage to things.

But there is another option, the transformation of life through religious creativity — the achievement of what culture attains only in symbols and civilization not at all. Berdyaev wrote of three epochs in the drama of God and man. The Hebrew vision of God as sovereign is succeeded by the age of redemption, when men recognize the immanence of what was originally believed transcendent. Christ discloses the divinity of man. In the age of the Spirit, man will employ his freedom to participate fully in the creativity of God. He will exercise his divine vocation — theurgy.[49] In his early books, Berdyaev was convinced of the imminence of the age of the Spirit. In later years the final epoch seemed to him far away in the future. But always the idea of theurgy remained the standard by which to interpret creativity and the ultimate hope for it.

These divergent themes, the vision of the limitless potential of man's liberty and the anguished recognition of the fetters still upon it, Berdyaev never reconciled. The darker note resounds through his later writings: intending to bring this world to its end and regain paradise, men can bring forth from their freedom only symbols of that unattainable reality, symbols that tantalize by their insubstantiality, for the power of the fallen world is not overcome. Theurgy becomes less the way by which man will inaugurate the Kingdom of God, more the way of life he will lead within it. But all creativity is at least a prophecy of the Kingdom. The values that emerge from it contribute to the Kingdom and will be conserved forever within it. History is even now the eighth day a creation, obscure testimony that man is a *microtheos,* a creator like the creative God. His activity is divine.[50]

THE ARTIST'S VENTURE

"Artistic creativeness," Berdyaev said, "best reveals the meaning of the creative act."[51] But why should men spend their time and passion on the arts if expression always means the distortion of creative intuition, if art simply augments the mass of the fallen world, if every artifact is a betrayal of the revolutionary ontological intention of the creative impulse? Berdyaev offers a variety of answers. First, art does not mean seeing, but doing. It is not a process of imitation, passive and contemplative, concerned with observation of the world. It rejects all that is visible and tangible for what no eye has seen nor ear heard. In the realm of imagination, a transfigured world is born that does conform to the exigencies of man's liberty. In its repudiation of this world, art is an avowal of human freedom and a protest against man's present bondage.

Secondly, though it achieves no more than a symbolic transformation of the world, art is still a token of man's proper destiny, a prophecy that can sustain and inspire those who have not fallen wholly under the spell of objectification. Thirdly, the meanings and values that emerge from the artist's venture would never be actualized in any other way, for man's creativity is the legacy of the *Ungrund.* What the artist does is a response to the divine appeal for assistance to actualize the good and transfigure the tragic possibilities of primordial freedom. What he does shapes the future character of the human enterprise and forestalls its return to barbarism. Fourthly, all his achievements are caught up into and are constitutive of the Kingdom of God, the plenitude of all value. Finally, the artist's venture is a quest for beauty. Beauty is an eschatological affair: not only does all that is beautiful belong to eternity, the eternal alone is truly beautiful.[52] But if the artist cannot create beauty itself, he does create symbols of it, and these epiphanies are never gratuitous. Whenever the quest for beauty is rewarded, this world has been momentarily transcended and the truth man's destiny does not lie within the realm of Caesar that has been affirmed.[53]

When Berdyaev writes of art as symbolic, his principal meaning is not that it offers images that illuminate the human condition in some profound and discriminating way. A work of art is a symbol simply because it is an artifact. There is no intrinsic reality to the natural, objective, and historical. He described the world of objects as " only the ' symbolization ' of the inner states of the spiritual world, that is, of its hatred and divisibility, and . . . not a substance existing by itself." [54] The artist's venture is symbolic because it cannot realize the ontological aspirations of the creative impulse.[55] But there is another facet to his reflections on symbolism which led him to ascribe a certain messianic function to the artist.

Only the symbolic consciousness which knows the distinction between appearance and reality can make sense of this world. To the realist it must appear ultimately absurd. The arts contribute to man's redemption because they affirm that all things in time and space are only images and shadows of what is divine. Art is not only a witness to freedom but a way toward it as well, for art always protests against the banal realism that confirms man in his servitude to the realm of objects. The artist's venture offers a road leading back from the brink of meaninglessness; it tells men that

the meaning of one world is to be found in another, and that this meaning itself is revealed to us in the latter. . . . Our natural empirical world does not possess in itself either significance or orientation; its qualities are dependent upon the extent to which it functions as a symbol of the spiritual world. . . . Everything which possesses meaning in our life is but the index and symbol of another world in which alone that significance inheres.[56]

When Berdyaev writes of the symbolic character of the artist's venture, he means to stress its tragic nature. When he writes of it as the consummate expression of the symbolic consciousness, he is concerned with its liberating and redemptive power. Although nothing finite is more than a symbol, authentic art is distinguished from all else because it exerts no false claim about its own reality, but is an exposure of the symbolic nature of all things that do.

Symbolic and realistic, romantic and classical, expressionistic and canonic — for Berdyaev these contrasts express the distinction between authentic and inauthentic creativity. He identifies all genuine art with expressionism, by which he means the disclosure of man's anguish at his confinement within the realm of objectification:

I could never escape the feeling of anguish when confronted with life in its inexorable finality, and always believed that man's stature and significance is in proportion to that in him which breaks through to infinity. . . . Burial is the most fitting thing that can happen in the finite world. . . . Religious anguish involves longing for immortality and eternal life, for redemption of the finitude of existence. Similarly, art appeared to me as imbued with anguish and, therefore, as evidence of the longing for transcendence. The magic of art is its power to wrench out the roots of finitude and to turn man's gaze to the eternal.[57]

Canonic art is pagan, seeking refuge in form and law from the limitless possibilities of freedom. The visual arts, especially sculpture, are intrinsically pagan. Music is the most romantic form of the artist's venture, and so most appropriate for the expression of the Christian vision. Berdyaev contrasts pagan and Christian art in this vein:

The heavens are closed above pagan art and the ideals of perfection are of the here and now, rather than of the beyond. Only in pagan art do we find that classic perfection of form, that immanent attainment of beauty in this world, by the means of this world. . . . There is no upsurge towards another world: this attained perfection closes man in this world. . . . Christian art is of another spirit. Heaven opened above the Christian world and revealed the beyond. In the art of the Christian world, there is not, nor can there be, a classic finality of form, immanent perfection. . . . In this world only a striving toward the beauty of another world is possible, only the longing for that beauty. . . . In pagan art there was classic health. Christian art is romantically ailing.[58]

He was particularly fascinated by the Quattrocento and Botticelli, whose art disclosed to him most intensely the dimensions of the conflict between pagan and Christian. Botticelli, debtor to both traditions, portrayed the Christian story in a classical context. The two tempers struggle against one another and neither triumphs. If his Venuses have abandoned the earth, his Madonnas have abandoned heaven. Classical health has succumbed to romantic ailment. Yet the nostalgia his painting expresses is ambiguous; it seeks the restoration of the old health as well as the fulfillment of the new yearning. But what ultimately characterizes Botticelli is his inability to create " a perfect image of the Madonna in this terrestrial existence. . . . The Coming of Christ and the Redemption had invalidated the intrinsic perfection of creative forms." [59] Raphael and Baroque art, impressionism and every form of realism, Berdyaev calls anti-eschatological and inauthentic.[60] And the nineteenth century, except in Russia, was the worst of times. Despite the way he yokes expressionism and the Christian vision, for Berdyaev modern art represents the loss of any authentic image of man in the name of which to protest against the world's tyranny.

A CRITICAL POSTSCRIPT

There are two lessons that the work of Nicolas Berdyaev leaves impossible to ignore. One is that the theme of consummation can provide neither the exclusive nor the primary perspective for a Christian interpretation of the artist's venture. When it is divorced from the Genesis story of creation, eschatology is impoverished until it designates little more than " a revelation of a Kingdom which is not of this world and which signifies that there is no making out anything in this world." [61] This approach leads to a flawed analysis of the relation of creative impulse to expression, of the nature of finite freedom, of the role of the artist as rebel, of the connection between the artist's enterprise and man's ordinary commerce with the environment. The other lesson is that neither must the image of the cross entirely dominate a theological analysis. It does justice to neither God nor man. The themes of estrangement and redemption cannot invest the human venture with its full significance. They truncate the meaning of man's liberty and ignore the love of God manifest in the gift of a distinctive creaturely vocation. Berdyaev is right to argue that another perspective is necessary. This is his importance. But it must affirm faith in the Creator, not deny it. It must see more than the negative aspects of man's relation to nature. It must not divorce freedom and authentic creativity from man's response to the challenges of his environment.

The case for the integral relation between apprehension and expression, which Berdyaev's stance toward the world will not allow him to admit, has been argued in an earlier chapter. This is one fundamental motivation for what the artist does. He creates in order to discover the detail of the fabric of experience, and it is necessary to grasp that detail. But the question of freedom requires more attention. Does perfect freedom mean escape from all limits? Is this the freedom the artist seeks and is it affirmed at least symbolically in his work? Berdyaev never recognizes, except as a source of frustration and tragedy, the context that endows freedom with determinate possibilities so it can become more than arbitrariness and caprice.

He calls music the most romantic of the arts, the one that best expresses the meaning of freedom, creativity, and the Christian vision. Igor Stravinsky offers an interpretation of music diametrically opposed to what Berdyaev says. When he begins to compose, Stravinsky writes, he is terrified by an apparently limitless freedom and the feeling that " everything is permissible." But his terror vanishes when he remembers that:

I have the seven notes of the scale and its chromatic intervals at my disposal, that strong and weak accents are within my reach, and that in all of these I possess solid and concrete elements which offer me a field of experience just as vast as the upsetting and dizzy infinitude that had just frightened me. . . . What delivers me from the anguish into which an unrestricted freedom plunges me is the fact that I am always able to turn immediately to the concrete things that are here in question. I have no use for a theoretic freedom. Let me have something finite, definite. . . . My freedom will be so much the greater and more meaningful the more narrowly I limit my field of action. . . . Whatever diminishes constraint diminishes strength.[62]

Stravinsky insists that the musician, no less than the sculptor or the painter, is concerned with the finite and circumscribed. No matter what his medium, it is especially the artist who knows the values of physical reality, the services of limits and constraint.

Stravinsky cites Leonardo's statement that strength is born of constraint and dies in freedom. Is not the fugue, he asks, an instance of the composer's " submission to the rules? And is it not within those strictures that he finds the full flowering of his freedom as a creator? " [63] When belief that freedom is the principle of strength leads to the rejection of all limits, all that can be achieved is " the arbitrariness of whim and the disorders of fancy." [64] And if this is true for the composer, it is no less valid for the man of letters. " The secret of salvation," he continues, lies in Baudelaire's comment that

rhetorics and prosodies are not arbitrarily invented tyrannies, but a collection of rules demanded by the very organization of the spiritual being, and never have prosodies and rhetorics kept originality from fully manifesting itself. The contrary . . . would be infinitely more true.[65]

When the Christian theme of creation is abandoned for exclusive reliance on that of consummation, the result is an interpretation of freedom that contradicts what artists have to say of their own endeavor.

The argument that the artist's venture is a natural and necessary development from more primitive commerce with the world has also been advanced in another chapter. But if it is valid, what the artist does constitutes a response to the challenges of existence rather than an attempt to escape from them. This aspect of his enterprise must be appraised either in the context of the Genesis story of creation or else in a wholly negative way. Berdyaev rejects Genesis, defines art as the passion for eternity, and so must condemn as surrender to objectification the relation of the artist's venture to man's elemental need to discover more of the world around him. Realism is inauthentic. If art is not rebellion, it is not art. He insists it is not a *response* to what God has done, but a *participation* in the divine struggle to bring this world to an end.

But is any artist simply a rebel? Is his labor ever entirely the child of discontent? Then how is it possible to account for his concern with tactile values, all that is circumscribed and definite, with what James Joyce called " the ineluctable modality of the visible "? How is it possible to account for words like these of Picasso: " I get an indigestion of greenness. I must empty this sensation in a picture "? A poem by W. B. Yeats, " For Anne Gregory," captures the way the artist comes to the world:

> Never shall a young man,
> Thrown into despair
> By those great honey-coloured
> Ramparts at your ear,
> Love you for yourself alone
> And not your yellow hair.

> But I can get a hair-dye
> And set such colour there,
> Brown, or black, or carrot,
> That young men in despair
> May love me for myself alone
> And not my yellow hair.

> I heard an old religious man
> But yesternight declare
> That he had found a text to prove
> That only God, my dear,
> Could love you for yourself alone
> And not your yellow hair.[66]

The artist cannot forget how much of Anne Gregory is expressed in yellow hair. His gift is to remind us of all the yellow hair in the world. He pushes us so that we bump into things and see all the yellows and greens of life. He teaches us to recognize the truth, even if we do not respect the reverence, of a poem that Yeats called " A Prayer for Old Age ":

> God guard me from those thoughts men think
> In the mind alone;
> He that sings a lasting song
> Thinks in a marrow-bone.[67]

It is especially the writer and the painter who think in a marrowbone, for whom the way to wisdom lies through the senses, not beyond them. Whenever the artist uncovers the real contours of experience and gets to the guts of things, his talent discovers images that illuminate the human situation — images like that of the marrowbone. Berdyaev often writes of the symbolic character of things, but he never means that the symbol and what it points toward both have their own intrinsic significance and value. For him, the meaning of the symbol resides in its relation to what lies beyond it; it has little meaning in itself. Always, Berdyaev seemed to want the marrow without the bone. Certainly the artist is a rebel. He protests against the wanton spilling of the marrow from bones cruelly broken. But he protests because those bones support some yellow hair he knows and loves.

If this world is a cluster of images and shadows of another

one, whatever passion for ultimate reality that inspires must not blind men to the yellow things of the here and now. The best antidote for such blindness is what the artist does. That is what he says. Yellow.

It serves no purpose to criticize Berdyaev for his departures from the Christian tradition. They were deliberate and seemed to him wholly justified. If his vision demonstrates the limits of an eschatological perspective, it also contributes something essential to the theology of culture that neither Protestant nor Catholic traditions had ever so unambiguously affirmed. But because he deprives himself of the full resources of the Christian message, Berdyaev is forced to appraise the human enterprise in a way that finds little empirical corroboration. His interpretation of the artist's venture simply contradicts the evidence it supplies concerning its own origin and nature. And whatever dialogue means, it must mean more than this.

IV

ART AS RESPONSE
TO THE CREATOR

MARITAIN AND THE MEANING OF POETRY

The Thomist tradition provides a philosophy rather than a theology of art, for it distinguishes between the natural and the supernatural in a manner foreign to classical Protestantism. Faith alone offers man full access to the supernatural, but there are no restrictions on the competence of reason within its own domain, even though it may know nothing of the story of man's redemption. Grace does not destroy nature but fulfills it, and revelation does not contradict reason but tells of another realm. So the artist's venture can be interpreted without direct reference to revelation.

What is distinctive about the Catholic approach is the assumption that unaided reason can prove the reality of a transcendent Cause of all things and discover, in the form of " laws of nature," what that Cause requires of the world. God wills that the world should be and should be essentially as it is. He wills the existence and governs the activities of all the creatures that inhabit it. This Author of nature calls men to the fulfillment of the powers and exercise of the liberty he has awarded to them. The creative enterprise is one form of response.

The way the Thomist tradition approaches the arts is the third option for the theology of culture. It speaks of the generosity of the Creator, although this is gathered not from revelation but is the conclusion of philosophical reason. It affirms the independence of the secular as the other options do not, though at the peril of obscuring its interdependence with the religious. Like the other approaches, it can become so much concerned with a single perspective that it loses the full resources of the Christian vision.

Art is important because it gives pleasure, and more especially, writes Jacques Maritain, because of the particular kind of intellectual pleasure it gives.

" No man," says S. Thomas following Aristotle, " can live without pleasure. Therefore a man deprived of the pleasures of the spirit goes over to the pleasures of the flesh." Art teaches man the pleasures of the spirit . . . and from afar off, without thinking, it prepares the human race for contemplation (the contemplation of the Saints), the spiritual joy of which surpasses every other joy and seems to be the end of all human activities.[1]

Despite his suggestion that there are some affinities between aesthetic and mystical experience, Maritain is concerned to clarify their fundamental differences, not to describe the creative enterprise as the forecourt of religious awakening. One is natural and the expression of man's own powers, while the other is supernatural and the effect of divine grace. The artist's venture and the quest of the mystic are different because

poetry emanates from the free creativity of the spirit, it is from the very start oriented toward expression, and terminates in a word proffered, it wants to speak; whereas mystical experience, because it emanates from the deepest longing of the spirit bent on knowing, tends of itself toward silence and internal fruition. Poetic experience is busy with the created world and the enigmatic and innumerable relations of existents with one another, not with the Principle of Being.[2]

Art is a natural affair, in the sense that it is busy with the created universe and expresses a natural human ambition and elemental need. It is an attempt to intensify our cognitive commerce with the things of this world because their physical properties have limitless capacity to delight us. Art does not convey man's anguish at his bondage to the world so much as it does the power of finite and definite things to please his senses. So it is a kind of witness to the unity of all creaturely life: Maritain calls it a disclosure of the congeniality of man and the world. The Jesuit theologian William Lynch proposes the loving descent of Christ into the depths of the finite as a model for the artist's venture. Étienne Gilson describes painting as a revelation through man of the inner creative force everywhere at work in the realm of nature.

The religious significance of the creative enterprise lies in its implicit acknowledgment of the benevolence of God the Creator. He has established man in a world of such beauty that it inspires an aesthetic expression of creaturely freedom.

A classical work of art, a work of Bach, for example, creates order in man, evokes the order of the world, renders its laws comprehensible and even lovable. . . . Art is an exercise of the whole being of man, not to compete with God, but to coincide better with the order of creation, to love it better.[3]

Although the words were written by a Protestant, they capture the distinctive accent of Thomist accounts of what the artist does.

Perhaps no one else in this tradition is as influential today as Jacques Maritain. The title of *Creative Intuition in Art and Poetry* [4] reflects his two principal concerns. One is to defend the role of reason in the artist's venture. The arts emerge from the preconceptual life of the intellect, and what they convey is an obscure kind of knowledge that cannot be expressed in any other fashion. The other is implied in his definition of poetry. The creative imagination awakens only through commerce with the finite and definite ingredients of man's environment. It loses its power when it turns away from the visible and tangible and hovers above the earth. The arts present man and the world in their mutual inter-penetration and baffling entanglement. Maritain claims that all forms of aesthetic expression, no matter how different in other ways, share one characteristic — poetry. He uses the word not in its ordinary sense but to describe an "inter-communication between the inner being of things and the inner being of the human Self which is a kind of divination." [5] Such poetry is "the secret life of each and all of the arts." [6]

Oriental and Occidental art are very different in the ways they approach man and the world. Oriental art is entirely intent upon things. Its creators do not attempt to express their own subjectivity. Instead, they seek to commune with things in themselves. But Chinese and Indian art still bear very little similarity to each other. The source of their difference does not lie in the things man contemplates but in the men who contemplate. Even art that is entirely concerned with the portrayal of things in themselves discloses the creative subjectivity of the artist. Indeed, the more it penetrates the interiority of things, the more it bears the stamp of the sensibility of its author. [7]

Western art has become less engrossed with the world, more concerned to express the imaginative powers of the self. Even so, Maritain writes:

To the very extent to which art has been really able to reveal and express creative subjectivity, to that extent it also, and by the same token, has been busy revealing and expressing the secret aspects and infinitely varied meanings of Things.[8]

Contemporary painters in the West do not often attempt to represent the surfaces of things in their art, but neither have they turned away from the physical universe. As they have explored the depths of their own creative powers, their subjectivity has itself " become the very vehicle to penetrate into the objective world " and discover there " the same kind of inner depth and inexhaustible potentialities for revelation as the Self of the painter." [9] The last hundred years have been a time of exceptional artistic creativity, for

on the one hand never was painting so purely painting, and on the other hand never in painting was such poignant humanity united with such powerful penetration of visible things, through the simultaneous manifestation of the painter's creative Self and of the occult meanings grasped by him in reality.[10]

Important as the differences are between the arts of Occident and Orient, what they have in common is much more important. Art intent upon the world reveals the self as well. Art intent to express the self also discloses something of the nature of the world. In what the artist creates, there is always a certain commingling or interpenetration of self and world. Each remains what it is, " it keeps its essential identity, it even asserts more powerfully this identity of its own, while it suffers the contagion or impregnation of the other. But neither one is alone." [11] This is poetry, this strange mixture of subject and object in which the integrity of neither is lost. Its presence in all art leads Maritain to believe the artist's venture involves a unique way of knowing. This form of cognition in which self and things are grasped together, in and through one another and inseparably united, is creative intuition. It has no parallel in logical reasoning, in the ventures of scientists or philosophers, although it has equal title to be described as cognitive.

For those of Maritain's philosophical persuasion who stress the objective character of knowledge, to know means to become, in an immaterial and spiritual way, that which is known. Ideas play an instrumental role in this union, but ideas are cognitive instruments and not cognitive objects. What the intellect grasps are not ideas of reality but reality itself, conveyed to the intellect by means of ideas. What is known exists independently of the mind and is apprehended in its own stubborn independence, " *as something other,* as free from me." [12] Maritain writes:

At the instant when it knows, the intellect is, immaterially, the object itself; *the knower in the act of knowing is the known itself in the act of being known;* before knowing, our intellect is like a formless vitality, waiting to be shaped; as soon as it has received from the senses, by means of its own abstractive power, the intelligible impression of the object, the intellect becomes that object, while carrying it, through the concept it produces of it, to the ultimate degree of formation and intelligible actuality, in order at the same time to raise to the supreme point its own immaterial identification with the object. [13]

Creative intuition is not an impure form of knowledge. This immaterial identification with what is known still occurs, but in such a way that it is also revelatory of the self.

Self and world are disclosed together because of the crucial role that emotion plays in this cognition. It is emotion that transcends " mere subjectivity, and draws the mind toward things known and toward knowing more." [14] It affords the creator access to the nature of things. It enables him to see. It has become *intentional.* Intentionality refers to the way what is known is present in the instrument by which it is known — a fire engine in the idea of the fire engine. In creative intuition, the world is grasped through emotion which has become as intentional as ideas are in ordinary cognition. But self and world are entangled because such emotion transcends the subject-object polarity on which other forms of knowledge are based. What the artist knows he does not grasp

in the ordinary sense of the word to know, but by receiving all this into the obscure recesses of his passion. All that he discerns and divines in things, he discerns and divines not as something *other* than himself, according to the law of speculative knowledge, but, on the contrary, as inseparable from himself and from his emotion, and in truth as identified with himself.[15]

As emotion supplants idea in poetic knowledge, so do artifacts supplant concepts in poetic expression. What the creator knows eludes conceptualization and can be communicated only through his art.

Maritain tells us that creative intuition might best be described as knowledge through connaturality. He refers to Thomas Aquinas' distinction between two ways men can be acquainted with virtue. We can read moral philosophers until we know all there is to know about the virtues, and still have none of them. On the other hand, we can be hopelessly ignorant of moral philosophy and still possess them all. Then we know the virtues by congeniality or connaturality, " by looking at and consulting what we are and the inner bents or propensities of our own being." [16] Such knowledge through affective union is what is involved in creative intuition, when a man suddenly encounters the world " actually as a part of himself." [17]

Always creative intuition " is directed toward concrete existence as connatural to the soul." [18] Imagination is empty and sterile until it is filled with " some complex of concrete and individual reality, seized in the violence of its sudden self-

assertion and in the total unicity of its passage in time." [19]
Maritain is committed to the theory of art as imitation, by
which he does not mean the representation of the surfaces of
things but the exploration of their inner workings. Talent
must put down roots into the earth if it is not to die. The
artist's venture derives its life from the connaturality to which
it testifies between man and the individual existents that
populate his world. On abstract art Maritain comments that

if it is true that creative subjectivity awakens to itself only by simultaneously awakening to Things . . . and that poetic intuition
is nothing but the grasping of Things and the Self together
through connaturality and intentional emotion — then it must be
said that in breaking away from the existential world of Nature,
from Things and the grasping of Things, . . . any effort to express freely the free creativity of the spirit, and to reveal the depths
of creative subjectivity is bound to slow extinction. [20]

Artists are people who make things that arrest and please
the senses. Beauty is not the goal of the creative enterprise,
Maritain writes, but only a transcendental correlative, and
an end beyond any end. [21] Beauty is a " kind of gift from
above " which a work of art possesses simply because it is " a
thing produced, and results from its participation in the
transcendental order of beauty." [22] It is transcendental attribute of Being: whatever is, is beautiful, even though man's
flawed vision cannot always discern the beauty resident in all
existing things. Art is beautiful, not because its author has
sought to make it so, but simply because it has been brought
into existence within the world God has created and affirmed,
sustains and governs. The aesthetic appeal of paintings and
poems is a particular determination of this transcendental or
ontological beauty — it delights the senses and the intellect
together. The pleasure these things afford is related both to

their sense values and also to " an *intellectual gift,* a participation in the poetic knowledge and poetic intuition through
which the poet has perceived a certain unique mystery in
the mystery of the world." [23]

But poetry has much of the significance that Maritain as-
cribes to it, and requires a special kind of intuition as its
source, only for one who is committed to the way that Thom-
ists understand the nature of knowledge. In an earlier chapter, a different interpretation was offered. *What* we experience is organized in a distinctive manner because it is *we* who
experience it. If experience tells us something of the nature
of the world, it also tells us something of the nature of those
who have the experience. The creative and interpretive powers of the mind enter the knowledge process from its first moments. Words and ideas are themselves part of the stuff with
which intellect always works, because only through their
agency is experience carved up and sorted out so that it is at
the disposal of the mind. Self and world are always entangled.

The reverse is also true. Self-expression involves an obscure
disclosure of the world, for emotions do not arise in a vacuum.
Passio means being acted upon, a suffering of things. As we
grasp the character of our affective lives, we also learn something of the universe we inhabit. The trouble with the distinction between brute feeling and intentional emotion is
that emotions do provide a sort of acquaintance with what
exists beyond the self, even if they do not afford us such pure
access to the nature of things as Maritain suggests. The interpenetration of things and the self in the artist's venture suggests a unique cognitive process only in the context of a realistic theory of knowledge. Perhaps the arts are no more than
a vivid witness to the inescapable limits of all knowledge.
Perhaps the creative enterprise would be better described as

a particularly intense and discriminating instance of our
ordinary commerce with the world.

Creative Intuition in Art and Poetry not only examines a
way of knowing, it also implies a way of being, for the world
is known " through union or inclination, connaturality or
congeniality." [24] But the artist's venture sometimes furnishes
scant evidence for this. The world has a sort of Janus face,
and contemporary art tells of the torments of the human condition when the world turns its darker visage. In our novels
and drama, the universe seems brutal and enigmatic and its
acquaintance breeds recoil. Kafka's account of the metamorphosis of Gregor Samsa, Sartre's portrayal in *No Exit* of
the ubiquity of hell, O'Neill's rehearsal of the Last Supper in
The Iceman Cometh — these give us man lost not because
he has left his home but because there is no home, betrayed
not at the hands of friends or ultimate power but because
community is impossible and of ultimate power there is no
trace. Contemporary literature brims with images of the
stranger and the voyager, the loner forever exiled from the
comfortable landscape of old moral and religious visions. Its
populace has heard what Jupiter says to Orestes in Sartre's
drama *The Flies:* " You don't belong here, intruder. You are
in the world like a splinter in the flesh."

Maritain does little justice to the ambivalence of the creative enterprise, the way an artist's consent to the world and
celebration of it is accompanied by a gesture of protest, a rejection of the present shape of things. In his discussion of
creative intuition, he writes:

There is no conflict or break between senses and reason, because
there is no division. . . . This place is the only one that is not
wounded, I would say, by the old hereditary sin which wounds
human nature. It is a kind of earthly paradise. [25]

But not all art, nor all the best of it, springs from a paradise where the loneliness and estrangement of life are unknown, sense and reason still united, self and world known in their interpenetration and congeniality.

The New Testament speaks of elemental powers of the universe to which man is in bondage.[26] Their tyranny has been broken in principle by the work of Christ, but though his victory is real it is not yet wholly realized. The disrupted world still waits for its redemption to be fulfilled. In the letter to the Romans, Paul writes of the fall of creation and its participation in man's estrangement:

For the creation waits with eager longing for the revealing of the sons of God; for the creation was subjected to futility, not of its own will but by the will of him who subjected it in hope; because the creation itself will be set free from its bondage to decay and obtain the glorious liberty of the children of God. We know that the whole creation has been groaning in travail together until now; and not only the creation, but we ourselves, who have the first fruits of the Spirit, groan inwardly as we wait for adoption as sons, the redemption of our bodies. (Rom. 8:19 ff.)

These lines express a Christian conviction that is absent from, or at least obscured by, Maritain's approach. In the artist's protest against whatever conspires to deprive man of his humanity, there is some corroboration of what Paul writes — if not of the hope he expresses, certainly of the way he sees the world. The symbol of creation must be supplemented by those of cross and consummation to render a satisfactory account of the artist's venture.

The value of *Creative Intuition in Art and Poetry* lies in its recognition that every artist is very like Antaeus, the wrestler who was invincible while he touched the earth, his mother, but who died at the hands of Hercules when he was lifted off the ground. Art is anchored in the finite and definite, telling not of another world but of the powers this one has to delight the senses. If it speaks of the squalor and disruption of life, it is also a witness to the unity of self and world and to the beauty of things. The artist and the mystic go different ways. The creative enterprise is a kind of celebration of what God has made. It is one independent form of human activity, serving no other, and there is no way to appraise it well except in terms of its own internal laws and requirements.

In *The Responsibility of the Artist,* a later work on the autonomy of art, Maritain argues that it must not be subjected to either religious or utilitarian demands which violate its own integrity.

Artistic value and moral value belong to two different realms. . . . The painter may damn himself, painting does not care a straw, if the fire where he burns bakes a beautiful piece of pottery.[27]

An artist is always more than an artist, however; he is by nature a moral and social creature. So the autonomy of his venture is limited by the exigencies of the common good of the community, difficult though it may be to specify what those exigencies are.

As used by man's free will art enters a sphere which is not its own, but the sphere of moral standards and values, and in which there is no good against the good of human life. . . . From the point of view of Art, the artist is responsible only to his work. From the point of view of Morality . . . the artist is responsible to the good of human life. . . . Thus, what we are confronted with is the inevitable tension . . . between two autonomous worlds, each sovereign in its own sphere. . . . They cannot ignore or disregard one another, for man belongs in these two worlds.[28]

But this does not mean that the artist is called to enlist in the service of church or state. His enterprise is distorted

whenever it is evaluated in terms of social utility or its power
to evoke religious fervor. The first principle of authentic creativity is that the direct responsibility of the artist is to his art
alone, and in it he discovers a master who demands absolute
devotion. Life is more or less unitary, so there is a relation between art and the realm of morality and religion. But the artist's venture is only indirectly and extrinsically subordinate
to this other province. Unless the "inevitable tension" between these autonomous worlds is accepted, the creative
enterprise will be "warped and bent to the service of a master
who is not its only genuine master, namely the work, its true
object, in the service of which it achieves its own inalienable
freedom." [29]

CHRIST AND APOLLO

Men want two things and are not willing to sacrifice either
one for the other. They want to find meaning and value, but
they are bound to what is visible and tangible and concrete.
They do not want "to go beyond them to get at meaning,
joy, or illumination." [30] They want earth and heaven, flesh
and spirit, time and eternity, the real and the ideal. The problem of the literary imagination is simply the problem of man:
how to reconcile these disparate ambitions and see the world
in a grain of sand. In *Christ and Apollo,* William F. Lynch
argues that the ascent to wisdom is only by way of a descent
into the actual texture of things, and proposes the passion of
Christ as a model for the artist's venture.

I mean Christ to stand for the completely definite, for the Man
who, in taking on our human nature (as the artist must) took on
every inch of it . . . in all its density, and Who so obviously did
not march too quickly or too glibly to beauty, the infinite, the
dream. I take Him, secondly, as the model and source of that

energy and courage we again need to enter the finite as the only creative and generative source of beauty.[81]

What Maritain argues concerning the way that creative intuition is oriented toward finite and definite existents is here transposed into an explicit theological key. But while both men write of the nature of the creative imagination, Lynch is especially concerned to discriminate between authentic creativity and flawed processes of imagination, and to chronicle the ways in which the latter damage the cohesiveness and inner logic of what they produce.

The exaltation of Christ came because of his humiliation and acceptance of all the limitations of finitude. He " moved down into all the realities of man to get to his Father." [32] So whether we believe in him or not, Christ " represents an ideal point at which the imagination can relax the strain of its double aspirations." [33] The way to wisdom, for the artist as for every man, leads through the finite and not away from it. " With every plunge through, or down into, the real contours of being, the imagination also shoots up into insight, but in such a way that the plunge down *causally generates* the plunge up." [34]

By Apollo, Lynch means the gnostic, the dreamer, the knight of the infinite, the man of timeless ideas who rejects the daily bread of experience in his search for meaning and value and " tries to get as much as possible of heaven out of as little as possible of earth, and even the little of earth [he] does touch is not taken seriously in a cognitive way." [35] When literature is created in the shadow of Apollo, the desires for meaning and for concretion are never truly reconciled. Imagery is simply exploited for illustrative purposes, or else it is at odds with the meanings that are finally affirmed. In neither instance do the intrinsic dimensions of the imagery lead to some sharpened vision of things. The descent and the ascent fall apart. The descent is broken off or else what it has mined is forgotten.

Christ and Apollo is primarily an examination of three forms of imagination — univocal, equivocal, and analogical. The univocal mind wants to comprehend the unity of things, and to achieve that ambition it " destroys or eliminates the variety and detail of existence." [36] It is content with a single dimension of self or world, with surfaces instead of depths. But what the univocal imagination does grasp is distorted because of its abstraction from all the other aspects of life. The stuff of experience is thrust into some confining mold that will convey a message or point of view. The univocal mind " does not respect reality; it exploits and uses it." [37] It does not linger with images and actions until they tell their own story, but employs them to illustrate an idea. It is impatient. Meaning is not allowed to emerge at its own pace in the course of time. Instead, it is grasped in a timeless instant. The passage of time is deprived of any intrinsic significance; it serves only to illustrate what has antecedently been affirmed.

The univocal imagination is always more or less didactic. Perhaps it could also be argued that it is particularly sympathetic to a naturalistic account of things. As it sees only a single dimension of the world, so does it often see only the surfaces of the self. It implies that the self can be comprehended in terms of the world, as though a person were only another object. In D. H. Lawrence's novel *The Man Who Died,* the univocal mind appears possibly at its most didactic and banal. It is at work in *The Iceman Cometh,* where Eugene O'Neill tells us that the self is only a bundle of pipe dreams, and that when men have lost their illusions, they have been robbed of all they have and all they are. And it seems to Lynch that *The Plague* is inspired by a univocal vision, because of the way Camus presents the human venture so rigidly in terms of an incessant and never victorious battle against pain.

The novelist calls for a holy act of rebellion against all the forms of pain in men; it is therefore a rebellion which really asks that all other causes, all other zeals and purposes, be liquidated down into the form of this single crusade. . . . But to raise the single flag of the opposition to pain would flatten out this whole human world, with all its pluralisms and profound oppositions.[38]

The equivocal imagination recognizes the infinite variety of life, but it discovers no kind of intrinsic unity. It finds no patterns in human experience and so it imposes them upon it. At some point the imagination recoils from experience and proceeds as though it were absolutely autonomous and could function independently of the actual character of things. Instead of organic development, there are two unrelated movements. Everything is what it is and is nothing else. Everything is alone and all connections are fashioned purely by chance. So metaphor is an arbitrary device. There is no causal or internal relationship between imagery and meaning; they remain forever outside each other.

The hiatus between John Steinbeck's naturalism and what Malcolm Cowley has called the " hortatory passages " in *The Grapes of Wrath* is one instance of the equivocal imagination at work. Another is the way Theodore Dreiser leaps from an exoneration of the Clyde Griffiths of the world, since they are too much the creatures of their environment to be responsible for what they do, to an affirmation of God. The piety neither conditions nor is derived from Dreiser's vision of the human situation. They are related only in an arbitrary and external manner. Lynch cites Graham Greene as another example of the equivocal temper, for in his work the reality of transcendent beauty seems to be implied by the inexhaustible evil and irremediable ugliness of this world. Meaning and value, if they are found at all, are found only on the far side of the endless shabbiness of life as we know it now.

If there is a sort of congruence between the univocal imagination and naturalism, there is a similar one between the equivocal temper and gnosticism. Although it was a protean affair, gnosticism always reflected man's nausea in the face of the finite and definite and offered some kind of escape to another realm. For the gnostic, there are two worlds, one as bereft of value and beauty as the other is replete with them, and they have no relationship to one another. Sometimes the disparity is disclosed in art by the externality of the relation between imagery and meaning. Sometimes it is transposed into an explicitly theological key. But never is there an integral relation between the ascent to wisdom and the descent into the stubborn detail and variety of existence.

"Somewhere in between" the univocal and the equivocal lies the analogical imagination. It neither surrenders diversity nor surrenders to it. Instead, it moves down into the depths of the finite until it can find unity within diversity, similarity hidden beneath variety, connections between what first seemed unrelated. "The task of real thought," Lynch writes,

and of the imagination too, is to organize the diversity of reality in unity, but in such a way that the diversity, which is a fact, still remains. But if one orders the real in such a way that the one, or point of unity, is still really outside the many, or the like outside the different, nothing very important has been accomplished. . . . You still have that with which you started; the contraries still stand outside of each other. . . . I should say that we must achieve some kind of *interpenetration* of unity and multiplicity, sameness and difference, a kind of interpenetration in

terms of which the two contraries become one and the same thing
— but " become " this only because existentially they have always
been it.[39]

The equivocal imagination is correct in its insistence that
things are what they are, that they all have their own ob-
durate individuality. But the search of the univocal mind for
unity no matter what the cost, its passion for clarity and intelligibility, also reflects an ineradicable human need.

The analogical imagination manages to reconcile these divergent orientations because it does not break away from the
descent through the finite in its quest for wisdom. Its reward
is the discovery of deeper dimensions in ordinary things, hidden levels that sometimes blaze with significance that illuminates the whole human landscape. Lynch cites the revelatory
power of those few drops of water lying on the cottage floor
in *Riders to the Sea:*

A movement of the finger or the lips can reverberate through all
the levels of awareness of man because it can tell of all of these
levels as they are present in the finger or the lips. There are lines
in Synge's *Riders to the Sea* where the men are carrying the dead
body of Bartley in on planks, and the water from the body leaves
a line of wet upon the floor. It tells, as other lines do not, the
whole pitiful story of the human race against all great bodies of
water, and it gives us in a visual instant the story of all tragedy,
of that which cannot be done by the finite when it confronts an
infinite.[40]

Perhaps the tension between Christ and Apollo and the different stances toward the world they represent might be
clarified by a work to which Lynch himself does not refer —
the involution of Christian and classical imagery in *A Portrait of the Artist as a Young Man.* Stephen Dedalus understands his own condition in terms of the labyrinth of Minos,
for he bears its creator's name. Ireland is the old sow that

eats its farrow, as the Minotaur devoured the pride of Athenian youth. Stephen determines to fly beyond the snares it has set to deprive him of his freedom, all its hollow-sounding voices and heaps of dead language. To Dublin he says *non serviam;* he will be Stephen Icarus, Stephen Lucifer, the brightest of the angels and the morning star. The images of flight and ascent find their climactic expression in the great epiphany on the beach when he recognizes his vocation as an artist: life and death, ascent and descent, soaring and falling, are violently juxtaposed.

But Stephen also describes the artist's venture in the language of the eucharist. He will be " a priest of the eternal imagination, transmuting the daily bread of experience into the radiant body of everliving life." [41] These two kinds of symbolism interpenetrate to disclose the youthful folly in Stephen and the perils that await him. He shakes off the cerements of Dublin. He is going to " create proudly out of the freedom and power of his soul . . . a living thing, new and soaring and beautiful, impalpable, imperishable." [42] But to soar beyond time and space and create the impalpable out of no resource but human freedom, this is not a true eucharist, but a flawed and gnostic rite, an invocation of Apollo, not of Christ. The ascent does not emerge from the eucharistic act but is at odds with and corrupts the stubborn insistence of the sacrament on descent, on chewing up the daily bread of experience, feeling it in the throat, smelling the odor of the wine.

When he murmurs, " In the virgin womb of the imagination the word was made flesh," [43] the emphasis on virginal perhaps suggests why we see Stephen's talent paralyzed in *Ulysses.* The artist does not create by parthenogenesis out of his autonomous imagination. It provides only the yeast for the dough of experience. Stephen is too much drawn to Icarus to be quite Dedalus. He is tempted to fly too far from the earth and too close to the sun, in regions where the imagination cannot live. The powers of transubstantiation are offered only to those who like to linger with the daily bread of things. In the eucharist, Stephen finds a symbol for the artist's venture that is perhaps more appropriate than any other could be. But progress from Icarus to Dedalus, apprentice to artificer, depends on fidelity to that image. Descent and ascent must form a single movement, not simply juxtaposed as they are in the epiphany on the beach, or related to one another in some external way. Lucifer can be a dangerous muse for the artist — not because he is fallen but because he is an angel.[44]

In the last chapter of *Christ and Apollo,* Lynch writes of Christ as " the creator and the actuality behind a new imagination and a new creation," [45] not simply as a model for what the artist does. The creative enterprise is a cognitive affair, an exploration of the hidden dimensions of finite and definite things. These are not flat; they have many levels, and ultimately a Christic one. The old order of things has been overcome by a new creation, " within which the one, single, narrow form of Christ of Nazareth is in process of giving *its* shape to everything." [46] Jesus of Nazareth is concrete and definite, an individual born at a particular time, in a particular place. But he is also the reality behind all other realities. His power is subverting and transforming the old creation, incorporating it into his risen life. This One is at work including the many in himself, yet with no violence to their own integrity and diversity. The form that shapes this new creation

is no longer an existence which becomes different in everything it touches, leaving only the proportion the same, the proportion between the act of existence and the possibility of the essence. Now the action is Christ, rigidly one person. . . .[47] He has subverted the whole order of the old imagination. Nor is this said in the sense that he replaces or cancels the old; rather, he illuminates it, and is a new level, identical in structure with, but higher in energy than, every form or possibility of the old.[48]

The Christian imagination is one that somehow can grasp this level of the interpenetration of unity and diversity. The new creation is the final ontological truth of all things, unifying and empowering them from within. Christ is not external to the many, like the spurious unities the univocal imagination finds. He is the fulfillment of creation, through whom the diversity and specificity of all finite things find their freest and most intense expression. This one individual, Jesus of Nazareth,

shall have his narrow personal march from Bethlehem to Calvary, but he is already having his great march, by dramatic generative analogies, through history. It is only progressively, after it has the unbreakable confidence that there is some essential Christic development in supernatural history, that the new imagination begins to assume the order of creation and to lift it into its own vitality. Thus Christ is water, gold, butter, food, a harp, a dove, the day, a house, merchant, fig, gate, stone, book, wood, light, medicine, oil, bread, arrow, salt, turtle, risen sun, way, and many things besides. . . . The old realities and metaphors of nature are being raised to the level of historical commitment, and are therefore surcharged with new poetical power, not less.[49]

The man of letters must follow where the man from Nazareth led, through all the twists and crannies and depths of the finite, for there is no path to the Father or to any kind of wisdom that does not involve " the penetration of the finite and the definite concrete in all its interior dimensions and according to all its real lines." [50] Art is a kind of eucharistic act; it depends upon the finite and the definite, what is limited and what is circumscribed. Only by rubbing up against these ordinary little things do we come to beauty or meaning or joy or anything else that answers the needs of creatures made from the dust of the ground. That is as it should and must be, if God has willed and created the universe and come among us in incarnate form. The man of letters teaches us to feel the texture of life and stay close to it in the quest for insight. For him to do this is enough. But sometimes he can also awaken us to the new life that courses beneath the countenance of the old.

PAINTING AND CHRISTIAN PHILOSOPHY

In *Painting and Reality*, Étienne Gilson describes the artist's venture as a collaboration between man and the stuff of the physical universe. Sometimes that stuff proves recalcitrant, but it always plays a creative role in determining what a painter will do and say. " Each kind of material," he writes, " requires a mode of treatment adapted to its own nature, and, in turn, this technique itself largely conditions the form and substance of the work." [51] The medium of the artist is never a neutral element. Not only does it influence what he does, it also affects the way others respond to his work. Our commerce with paintings is very different from our relationships with novels or poetry, because the former are made of pigments and canvas, not words. The first thing that an examination of the creative enterprise discloses is the enormous importance of material causality.

This sort of dialogue between man and nature is not primarily an intellectual or spiritual affair.[52] A painter is an artisan whose talent lies more in the wrist and fingers than in the mind. The hand does not work in servile subjection to the intellect; there is a certain spontaneity in what it does and in what the painter's eye demands that it should do. The creative act is inspired by "a sort of instinct" [53] and a "confused feeling of some painting to be done." [54] Citing a statement by Herbert Read that "aesthetic activity is biological in its nature and functions," Gilson emphasizes the biological affinities between the conception and birth of paintings and of all living creatures. He tells us that in their comments on their own work, contemporary painters recognize the biological character of their venture. Many share the ambition

to bring art closer to nature than it seems to have been ever since, considering itself a sort of speculative approach to truth, it began to take sides with knowing against making. Many painters now tend to consider themselves natural forces sharing in the fecundity of nature and their works so many beings produced by nature through their own art.[55]

But it is not in the representational character of art that the relationship between painting and nature lies. It exists only in the similarity of their modes of operation. Modern artists are not concerned with the representation of anything that already exists. They seek to create objects worthy of existence for their own sake and whose entire significance "lies in themselves rather than in their relation to things." [56] Gilson insists that art means novelty, the creation of what no one would ever see unless the talent of the painter had produced it. It is born out of "fantasy, imagination, fiction." [57] A painting is not a referential device that points to something beyond itself. It is not an "image of a reality, but the reality of an image." [58]

All its ingredients are fused so that nothing is extraneous to the meaning of the whole. Nothing possesses any kind of referential value or independent life of its own: "Everything is determined to an artistic mode of existence." [59] Everything exists only for the sake of the total impact of the work.

When it is pasted on a canvas by a painter, a piece of newspaper loses its newspaperly nature; physically the same, it no longer exists as a piece of newspaper, but as a part of painting. It is painting.[60]

Form is what unites diverse elements and makes a painting out of them. It invests them with organic significance. Because of it, these lines and contrasts and colors no longer " mean " anything whatsoever except the formal visual experience they afford the beholder.[61]

Paintings are distinguished from all else because they have no function except to please the eye. They are created and valued simply because certain forms and colors capture our attention.[62] Even what is apparently representational art has always been organized in accordance with some notion of visual pleasure.[63] So painters can be described as people who do not find in nature

a certain class of objects that ought to be there — namely, objects whose existence, essence, and structure are exclusively justifiable by the pleasure found in apprehending them. . . . Because they do not find in nature objects whose exclusive *raison d'être* is the aesthetic pleasure derived from their perception, artists set out to produce such objects.[64]

But though art galleries are " palaces of pure pleasure," the delight that a painting offers is not brute pleasure but cognitive joy. Painters are concerned with the infinite variety of intelligible relations in the realm of the visible. They explore new ways in which this qualitative universe can give pleasure both to senses and to intellect. The source of the delight they afford us lies in the " very intelligibility of being." [65]

Gilson writes that philosophers have much to learn from painters. One who is acquainted with the artist's venture knows " the closest analogue there is, in human experience, to the creative power from which all the beauties of art as well as those of nature ultimately proceed. Its name is Being." [66] Paintings are made out of the stuff of the physical universe. But as paintings, not simply artifacts, they are " so many creations *ex nihilo.*" [67] The form that the artist has devised endows all the ingredients of his work with a new mode of existence. Gilson tells us that " it is of the essence of a painting to be a self-signifying substance and an addition to the sum total of already existing reality." [68] What the painter does is " a particular instance of the general productivity of nature." [69] His work illuminates

what is happening to the whole of which he is a part. What happens in painters suggests the presence, at the origin of universal becoming, of an inner force of invention and creativity that, everywhere at work in the world of matter, achieves self-awareness in the mind of artists.[70]

Painters are notoriously unable to predict the future evolution of their art. The creative enterprise is full of uncertainties and surprises, developments the artist himself could not foresee, even though he leaves nothing to chance. No matter how careful his calculations, he does not know precisely what his work will be until it is finished. He " does not know how his will ultimately will decide " until all decisions have been made and he actually confronts what it is he has created.[71] " Just as previsibility attends determination," Gilson writes, " imprevisibility attends liberty." [72] The artist's venture represents " the most perfect kind of causality given in human experience " [73] and it is an irrefutable vindication of human liberty.

Process is real, nature is inventive, man is free — this is what painting tells philosophy. Man transcends the world but his art is a collaboration with it that continues " through man the creative activity of nature." [74] In his own distinctive way, Gilson bears witness to what Maritain calls the connaturality of things and the self. The last pages of *Painting and Reality* address the question of the relation of art and religion. The world participates in the creative power of its Author; all creatures imitate God in that they exist and are causes. In what the artist does, this resemblance is raised to its highest intensity.

In a created universe whatever exists is religious because it imitates God in its operations as well as in its being. If what precedes is true, art, too, is religious in its very essence, because to be creative is to imitate, in a finite and analogical way, the divine prerogative, exclusively reserved for HE WHO IS, of making things to be. . . . Each artist, then, while exerting his often anguished effort to add new types of beings to those which make up the world of nature, should be conscious of the resemblance between his finite art and the infinitely perfect efficacy of the divine power. All truly creative art is religious in its own right.[75]

The Creator has freely given to his creatures their own causal powers. Whether he knows what he does or not, the artist responds to a great invitation " to join in the praise of God by cooperating with his creative power and by increasing, to the extent that man can do so, the sum total of being and beauty in the world." [76]

Painting and Reality, unlike what Tillich and Berdyaev have written, is a fine affirmation of the autonomy of the artist's venture. It is a salutary warning against the kind of theological imperialism that is intent on construing the history of art as a direct disclosure of the voyage of the human spirit. But Gilson insists so strenuously on the independence of the creative enterprise that it is absolutely isolated from everything else. There are many ways in which painting can be appraised, and no single one seems to capture all that can be said. Gilson's rigorously ontological approach, his exclusive concern with painting as the creation of new being and with form as the constitutive element in this creativity, diverts attention from values other than plastic values and obscures one part of what art discloses about the relation of man to the world.

He argues that a painting does not refer to anything beyond itself: " When it acts as a substitute for language, a picture is not a painting." [77] There is a profound difference between art and illustration. Those who rely on the accuracy of their representation of things for the appeal of their work are scarcely true painters. When our interest in a work of art depends upon the subject it portrays, we are not really interested in it as a work of art. But if the distinction is important, it is far from absolute.

There is another side to the matter, and Louis Arnaud Reid expresses it well in *A Study in Aesthetics*:

Of course the painter is interested in the expressiveness of visual *forms*. But he is interested in their *expressiveness*. The forms are "significant." And what does a human face express more definitely than human character? Surely the artist has more before him than " lines, planes, and volumes." Surely, if he is not ridden by theories, he is interested in character . . . character plastically expressed in a face which interests him. If this interest can in some sense be called dramatic, it will not be true to say that the " dramatic " painter will give emphasis to ultra-plastic values, in the sense of values outside and independent of plasticity. Rather, psychological values will become apprehended plastically.[78]

Gilson's perspective is particularly appropriate for much contemporary painting, but what Reid recognizes is indispensable if we are to appreciate the work of countless other artists. There is no reason whatsoever why all painting should be forced to submit to a single standard, whether that of Reid or Gilson or anyone else. What is necessary, however, is the realization that some art illuminates what lies beyond itself without betraying its own nature as art. The formal values of Michelangelo's work reverberate with his sense of the beauty of the human body. Those of Rembrandt are resonant with his sense of the depths of the human personality.

Joseph Albers defined the content of painting as the " visual formulation of our reaction to life." [79] A painter offers us not only something to see but also a particular way of seeing. Our vision of things gains a new dimension and grows more intense. This new way of seeing is a distinctively human way; it is laden with a freight of emotional significance. Visual form has emotional import. Sometimes that form tells of the springtime of the world, sometimes of the winter of our discontent. De Chirico gave his paintings such names as *Melancholy and Mystery of a Street, Nostalgia of the Infinite, Melancholia, Anguish of Departure*. The titles are unnecessary. The power to evoke a haunted and threatening world lies in the composition of the paintings themselves, the strange and distorted forms that present the world in its terrible otherness from man.

In *The Rebel,* Camus cites Van Gogh's statement that " I believe more and more that God must not be judged on this earth. It is one of His sketches that has turned out badly." [80] Every artist, Camus continues, " tries to reconstruct this sketch and to give it the style it lacks." The treatment a painter imposes on reality, the extent to which it is transformed by his style, suggests to Camus the intensity of the artist's rejection of the world as it is. Certainly his comments are relevant to *Guernica*. It is, first of all, a venture in the creation of plastic forms. But these forms themselves convey what Tillich calls the " piece character " of the world, intimations of its rape by demonic powers for which man is no match at all. When *Guernica* was first exhibited, Picasso stated very strongly his own interpretation of it as a protest against the brutalities visited on man by the modern world.

Perhaps in a " pure " philosophy of art it would be possible to exclude such comments by artists concerning their own work, banish all values except formal ones, and ignore the emotional significance that visual forms somehow possess. But these considerations are certainly relevant for the theology of culture, for it is concerned not only to guard the integrity and independence of the creative enterprise, but also to interpret it in the wider context of man's relation to the world and to its Author. Gilson's stubbornly ontological approach demonstrates what the flaw is in the theological distinction between natural and supernatural. The two are finally deprived of almost any relationship to one another at all.

Gilson writes that painters are the creators of objects for which man has an irrepressible appetite but which do not exist in the world around him, objects whose only rationale is the pleasure they afford. Painting is a sort of humanization of things. Colors are transposed purely for visual effect, principles of imaginative selection are always at work, and limits are imposed where none exist in nature. Everything is reorganized to afford man greater pleasure. Simply in the formal aspects of this venture, there is expressed a certain ambivalence toward the world, a repudiation as well as a celebration. The world is not the way man would have it be. Sometimes the rejection erupts into the impassioned protest of a *Guernica*. Sometimes it is present only in a germinal fashion, implied in the reorganization of things so that they conform more satisfactorily to the exigencies of human sense and sensibility.

But art is always an implicit protest against the world be-

cause of what the world lacks. It does not give man quite the
pleasure he requires. It is full of mornings such as April 26,
1937, when the planes of General Franco appeared above the
town of Guernica. Yet art is always a protest launched on behalf of man and on behalf of the world he inhabits, else there
would be no incentive to create or to employ a medium that
celebrates so much the values of the physical universe. Whatever else it is, painting is a kind of hymn to the stuff out of
which the world is made. But it also is an obscure witness to
the relevance of the symbol of the cross and to the fallenness
of the world and man. Gilson tells us that art is a continua-
tion through man of the inventiveness of nature. But what
painting says of the world seems more ambiguous than this.
What else there is, the New Testament calls the bondage of
creation. Edvard Munch manages to express it in six words
he used to describe his own art — " I hear the scream in nature."

V

ART AND THE NATURAL

THE CELEBRATION OF CREATION

Tillich and Berdyaev both appraise the artist's venture in the light of man's estrangement from ultimate reality. Even though Berdyaev insists upon the importance of creativity, it is interpreted entirely from the perspective of the fallenness of the world. No Christian could find this an inappropriate context. But it is neither the only nor the primary one, although contemporary Protestant thought often assumes that it is. When Tillich and Berdyaev rephrase faith in God the Creator in terms of divine creativity they fail to capture the majesty and full significance of the Biblical story. To exist means to be fallen. But first of all it means to be called to fulfill existence. Neither of them is able to affirm that a deliberate divine decision lies at the origin of all things. So neither is able to state unambiguously that existence involves the call to fulfill existence.

Either it becomes impossible to say that God has willed for man a distinctive creaturely vocation, or else it must be expressed as Berdyaev does in terms of the transcendence of time and space. Berdyaev stands the artist's venture more or less on its head when he argues that works of art are not the fulfillment of the creative impulse, but the tragic distortion of its original pure spirituality. For Tillich, the relative auton-

omy and diversity of the various aspects of the human enterprise finally dissolve in a religious continuum that devours
everything. The secular he cannot affirm in its own independence and integrity.

The story of creation does not provide the exclusive perspective for a Christian interpretation of the creative enterprise, but it does afford the foundation for it. What the artist
does is one vital form of response to the divine call to fulfill
existence, necessary for the survival of human community.
Then, too, we value the arts for many reasons, but the sim-
plest is the most important: certain sounds and forms and
colors give us pleasure. Paintings and sculptures and symphonies are forms designed to please the eye or the ear. Art is
a kind of hymn to the sense values of the world around us.
This appeal may be deeply buried in a work that expresses
some terrible human anguish, but it is still there. No matter
what its author intends and no matter how vividly he portrays man's estrangement and the hostile visage which the
whole earth sometimes turns toward him, art is still a trap to
capture and delight sense and sensibility.

Everything conspires to require the interpretation of the
artist's venture first of all in the light of the image of creation
rather than cross or consummation. It is a collaboration with
nature that lives by its appeal to the senses and discloses the
importance of material causality. It is a search for wisdom
that explores the inner dimensions of the finite and definite.
It thrives on and acknowledges the significance of limits and
law, of everything circumscribed and concrete. It contributes
to our commerce with the world and with our own feelings,
because the ingredients of experience cannot be known as
well as they must apart from aesthetic activity. It is a vindication of human freedom and causal power. It is a kind of play,
ignorant of all that lies beyond itself, following its own in-

trinsic laws of development, yet teaching man the requirements of life together and instilling a sense of fairness and
respect for order.

We do not spend our intelligence and passion in the creation of the arts because we are fallen creatures. Nor do we
create new worlds in art because the actual world is a fallen
one. We do all this for the sake of life in this world, distinctively human life. It is natural and necessary for us. Art is an
antidote against any kind of superficiality, and perhaps
against superficial spirituality most of all. From a Christian
perspective, it might best be called *the celebration of creation*.

On the other hand, one reason for the creative enterprise
is that our environment does not display the intelligibility and
beauty for which we yearn. So we create new worlds that
conform more exactly to man's desiring, where experience is
not so ambiguous. Sometimes art seems less a celebration of
creation than an invocation of a primeval harmony now
known, if known at all, only through the sense of its loss.
Camus wrote that the artist is always a rebel, one who not
only affirms the world but also protests against its present
condition. Art is always a dialectical affirmation and negation of things as they are. In *The Rebel,* he says:

Art is the activity that exalts and denies simultaneously. " No
artist tolerates reality," says Nietzsche. That is true, but no artist can get along without reality. Artistic creation is a demand
for unity and a rejection of the world. But it rejects the world on
account of what it lacks and in the name of what it sometimes is.[1]

What Camus means is expressed in a different vein in
The Plague. Tarrou and Rieux are rebels, committed to fight-
ing against creation as they find it, but one evening they find
brief respite from the battle against disease when they go for
a forbidden swim. They cherish the memory of those few
hours at the harbor. They are rebels just because there are

others, such as the dead child Jacques Othon, who cannot swim with them and know the joy and momentary peace of " gazing up at the dome of sky lit by the stars and moon." [2] So it is that art rejects the world on account of what it lacks and in the name of what it sometimes is.

Because it says yes and no to life, imposing on the world a coherence and intelligibility which it actually lacks, there is reason to relate the artist's venture to Christian eschatology and the hope of a transformed heaven and earth. There is a protest implied in the form of every painting, for reality is " humanized," reorganized to afford greater visual pleasure. The emotion that art expresses often discloses man's ambivalence toward the world, and sometimes it is a cry of pure anguish. But the referend of aesthetic activity remains the world in which we live, no other one. The symbol of consummation is important primarily because it emphasizes the dialectical character of what the artist does. There is always a negation within and subordinate to the artist's affirmation. This is the first way the definition of art as the celebration of creation must be qualified: *it is a dialectical affair in which the yes is always accompanied by a no.*

There is a second qualification more difficult to phrase and best conveyed by myth. As the sand that measures his last rational moments slips through the hour glass, Adrian Leverkühn, whose music held endless power to exalt and please, tells his friends:

Already since my twenty-first year I am wedded to Satan and with due knowing of peril, out of well-considered courage, pride and presumption because I would win glory in this world, I made with him a bond and vow. . . . For I well thought that he that will eat the kernel must crack the nut, and one must today take the divel to favour, because to great enterprise and devises one can use and have none other save him.[3]

Mann scarcely intends to convince us that there are powers of darkness at work in the world, or that Leverkühn's years of genius were bought from the Devil at the price of his soul. But he does portray how the peace and joy of a man's life can be drained away by the exigencies of his art. Creation can mean suffering, not ecstasy. Why is there so much testimony to the anguish of the artist's venture? Perhaps the answer is that in it men can confront the terror of nothingness.

There is some truth in the worn theory of an analogy between the creation of art and the activity of God the Creator. The similarities tell of the beneficence of God and account for something of the artist's pain. Men do not create out of nothing as God does. They need wood or words or the notes of the scale and its chromatic intervals. A work of art is never a monologue; always it is the product of a dialogue between some man's talent and the possibilities of his particular medium. But God has willed the existence of what is other than himself, and he is not jealous of the creatures he has made. He offers men their own opportunity to encounter the mystery of creation and to produce what did not exist before.

What the artist creates is more than the sum of its parts. The materials at his disposal condition what he can say and the aesthetic form he creates has no existence apart from them. But nothing precisely determines what that form should be. Its paternity cannot be chronicled. It has emerged from nowhere, from freedom, from the realm of pure possibility, midwifed by the talent of the artist. All the ingredients of an artifact undergo a metamorphosis because of it and henceforth they derive their life and significance from it. Gilson cites Constable's insistence that the business of the painter is "to make something out of nothing" and comments:

Among painters themselves, some perfectly sober minds do not hesitate to speak of their works as of so many creations *ex nihilo*. And, indeed, *insofar as its artistic mode of existence alone is at stake,* nothing of it is given to the painter in natural reality.[4]

The artist's venture is a particular kind of exploratory voyage to chart the farthest reaches of man's freedom. The anguish it involves is the sort of vertigo that an infinitude of possibilities inspires. Stravinsky writes of his dizziness before the abyss of liberty without constraint. Potentiality bereft of structure or character is a wasteland, and breeds " a sort of terror when, at the moment of setting to work and finding myself before the infinitude of possibilities that present themselves, I have the feeling that everything is permissible to me." [5] He speaks of the importance of the finite and definite, of limits and constraint, and of the guidance they offer him. But though man's creativity requires a medium, nothing completely determines the form that will elevate the medium to art and produce a new reality. The suffering of the artist points toward the generosity of God in awarding man the opportunity to engage in activity analogical to His own. This encounter with nothingness is the dark aspect of existence in the image of the Creator. It testifies that God does not begrudge man his privilege to bring into being what was not. This is the second qualification of the definition of art as the celebration of creation: *it can be an anguished hymn sung in the shadow of nothingness, for it is analogical to God's creation ex nihilo.*

There is another dimension of the analogy as well, another way the artist confronts what the Biblical mythology calls *Tohu Wabhohu,* the primal mystery which the Creator repudiated, chaos and darkness. The *Tohu Wabhohu* continues to exercise a kind of ghostly power, evident in all language that serves to obscure rather than to clarify the actualities of experience. It has been overcome by a divine fiat, and yet men can succumb to it or even invoke its power still. The prophet Jeremiah had a dream in which the Genesis story of creation was turned upside down and everything was swallowed up by chaos again:

> My anguish, my anguish! I writhe in pain! . . .
> I looked on the earth, and lo, it was waste and void;
> and to the heavens, and they had no light. . . .
> I looked, and lo, there was no man,
> and all the birds of the air had fled.
>
> (Jer. 4:19a, 23, 25.)

Experience is without form, and darkness lies on the face of the deep until it is transfigured by man's aesthetic activity, especially his use of language. But the darkness can return. Jargon and stereotypes and clichés bring it back. The artist's venture is a struggle against the specter of *Tohu Wabhohu,* and out of the exigencies of this some of its anguish comes. There is a certain similarity between the way our words are constitutive of our experience and the way the divine Word is constitutive of what we experience. Vivas phrased it in this fashion:

We ought not to obfuscate the fact that the world of affairs with its furniture is a world we grasp by means of an initial creative act of the mind which is in essence identical with the aesthetic vision, and that it remains distinct and fresh and blushing with the hues of value because the poet in us will not down. . . . Before the poet comes along the earth, for us, is without form and void. . . . If it were not for him, we would never see it.[6]

But the analogy between human and divine creativeness is very limited, for art remains a celebration of what God has made. What it conveys to us is the world we inhabit, with a little of the darkness that clouds conventional experience dispelled. It is a response to the triumph the Creator achieved over *Tohu Wabhohu*. It introduces us to the meanings and values of this world, and this is the one which God created and approved. But man has marred it, and that is reason enough why art should involve both a yes and a no. The man of letters participates most fully in the divine victory over chaos when he is a rebel, protesting against the present shape of things, the squalor and ugliness and dysteleological aspects of existence, in the name of what the world might be and man someday become.

The Biblical image of creation provides the foundation for an interpretation of the artist's venture. But the theme of consummation emphasizes its ambiguous and dialectical character. The story of the cross stresses the necessity for principles of discrimination by which to appraise it, for the fallenness of man is involved in his creativity as well as in all else he does. What are these standards and whence are they derived?

THE IDEA OF "THE NATURAL" AND ITS IMPORTANCE

In *Christ and Culture,* Richard Niebuhr writes that Catholicism expresses

a principle that no other Christian group seems to assert so well but which all need to share; namely, the principle that the Creator and the Saviour are one, or that whatever salvation means beyond creation it does not mean the destruction of the created.[7]

The God who comes to redeem man in Jesus of Nazareth is the Author of nature. So obedience to Christ involves fulfillment of the requirements that evolve from the nature man has been given. Created a social animal, man is called to elaborate social organization, procreate children, establish political and economic structures. If the advent of the Redeemer discloses the sinfulness and rebellion of man, it also testifies that the human venture cannot be identified with sin and rebellion, as the gnostics would do. Revelation in Christ means not only the judgment but also the affirmation of cultural activity.

But if the human enterprise is to be truly human, its laws cannot be based on the will of the strong. They must be faithful to the intention of the Creator. The Catholic tradition claims man can grasp that divine design. It is expressed in the form of natural law, which simply means that all things are called to affirm and achieve the ends entailed by the nature they have been given. All things are subject to natural law, but man alone has been given the opportunity to affirm it freely and deliberately. What it means for man is that he has a structure he cannot violate with impunity. It designates "the ensemble of things to do and not to do which follow . . . in *necessary* fashion" from the nature of man as man.[8] Natural law is unchanging, valid always and everywhere. But it is not a revealed law. So its import cannot easily be discerned. Often its meaning is distorted and misunderstood, because "our sight is weak, our nature coarse, and . . . innumerable accidents can corrupt our judgment."[9] Still, it furnishes Catholicism with an important standard for the appraisal of all human activity. Its virtue is that it does not derive from revelation and therefore should be universally acknowledged. It is related to the Christian belief in a Creator but in no way to the cross.

Protestantism has usually been skeptical of the idea of natural law. Reason is shaped by historical and cultural circumstances, and what seems universal one day appears provincial the next. There is an element of self-interest involved in our reasoning which leads us to exaggerate its purity and lack of bias. Our passion to serve eternal values becomes an avowal of the eternal significance of our own particular values, and the way we confuse the two is a fair gauge of human folly. Our ambition to discover the laws of God becomes the attempt to justify our own standards by endowing them with some inviolable religious sanction. So we call them dictates of the Holy One of Israel.

The guidelines that can be derived "in necessary fashion" from the nature of man as man are empty, few, and poor. So we shovel the reigning standards of a particular time and place into a receptacle marked " natural law " and propose the whole barrel as the definitive expression of what is natural for every place and every time. Furthermore, it is the nature of man to transcend nature. Any theory based on some presumably unalterable requirements of human nature can very quickly violate the liberty that is a definitive human characteristic, stifle our creative powers and blunt our sensitivity to concrete moral situations.

Every time one begins with a distinction between natural and supernatural, one ends with their divorce. The affirmation of the autonomy of the natural deprives the demands of God of their radical character. They are relativized because they must compete with a multitude of other claims. And never content with a relative autonomy, the natural covertly advances the pretension to have no judge beyond itself at all. So the attempt to discriminate between natural and supernatural ends with a vicious quantification. The Christian is confronted with two poles he must somehow relate to each other. But like all the king's horses and all the king's men when they faced Humpty-Dumpty, he is wrestling with what will not be put back together again. The will of God loses its relevance for human life or is tamed and domesticated by its confusion with the mores of some limited and particular situation.

But from the perspective of classical Protestantism, there is a single but decisive objection to the Catholic interpretation of the natural. For Luther and Calvin, there was one proper subject of Christian theology — the person and work of the Mediator. The beginning and the end of Christian thought is the will of God as it is expressed through the Biblical witness to the words and deeds of Jesus of Nazareth. Because the Son of God has come into this world, bone of our bone and flesh of our flesh, what grounds are there for the distinction between natural and supernatural? The way of the first Adam means loneliness and death. The way of the Second Adam means community and life. The classical reformers did not interpret the theological enterprise in the quantifying way which assumes that it is an attempt to relate apparent antitheses like divine and human, eternal and temporal, sacred and profane, supernatural and natural, and adjudicate between their various claims. In Jesus of Nazareth all these cohere, and it is their juncture in him which is the substance of Christian thought. What is natural for man cannot finally be discussed in abstraction from the one man who achieved its true proportions.

But there are still good reasons for Christians to speak of the natural. Theology is impoverished by its absence. Nowhere is the poverty so evident as in recent Protestant attempts to develop a theology of culture — although what the natural means has gained new attention from Protestant writers ever since Dietrich Bonhoeffer pled for the idea in words now widely known:

The concept of the natural has fallen into discredit in Protestant ethics. . . . This meant a serious and substantial loss to Protestant thought, for it was now more or less deprived of the means of orientation in dealing with the practical questions of natural life. The significance of the natural for the gospel was obscured and the Protestant Church was no longer able to return a clear word of direction in answer to the burning questions of natural life. . . . Before the light of grace everything human and natural sank into the night of sin, and now no one dared to consider the relative differences within the human and natural, for fear that by their so doing grace as grace might be diminished. It was its treatment of the concept of the natural that demonstrated most clearly that this Protestant thought was no longer conscious of the true relation of the ultimate to the penultimate. The consequences of this loss were grave and far-reaching. If there were no longer any relative distinctions to be made within the fallen creation, then the way was open for every kind of arbitrariness and disorder, and natural life, with its concrete decisions and orders, was no longer subject to responsibility to God. The sole antithesis to the natural was the word of God; the natural was no longer contrasted with the unnatural. For in the presence of the word of God both the natural and the unnatural were equally damned. All this meant complete disruption in the domain of natural life. The concept of the natural must, therefore, be recovered.[10]

It seemed to Bonhoeffer that when existence is understood entirely in the context of man's estrangement and God's redemptive work, so that before divine holiness everything seems equally damned or equally a matter of indifference, the church has nothing to say relevant to the actual complexity of life. But there are vital distinctions between proper and improper uses of freedom, natural and unnatural relationships, legitimate and illegitimate forms of play. Too often the church has failed to clarify these things, done it in some thoroughly ham-handed way, or consigned its affirmations to die by the slow death of a thousand qualifications.

But the idea of the natural is neither the only way nor in itself an adequate way to express these distinctions. If criti-

cisms of the Catholic interpretation of its content are as valid
and damaging as Protestants believe, then no kind of mysterious alchemy will exempt the idea from criticism when
Protestants use it themselves. The content with which it can
be invested is very modest and can be expanded only at the
cost of transforming it from a normative to a merely descrip-
tive category. But its cruciality for Christian thought, and especially for the theology of culture, is not jeopardized by the
modesty of its content. Its real service is to guard an indispensable Christian affirmation about God and prevent the reduction of the Genesis account of creation to a sort of dubious
archaeological appendage to Christian faith. Its function is to
put down the gnosticism that is a perennial weed in the Protestant garden.

A curious example of theological irrelevance is the assumption that Christian appraisals of the human enterprise should
be concerned with its criticism to the exclusion of its justification. When tedium eats at the lives of people, relentlessly
compels them to an ever more destructive search for new
anodynes to ease their boredom, brings them face to face
with the terror of meaninglessness, it is not enough if the only
word from the Lord is a prophetic denunciation of idolatry.
When people do not know where they stand, when clarity
of vision has succumbed to confusion before the awful complexity of things, the most debilitating kind of preaching is
that which tells of some fantastic paradise and offers, instead
of authentic existence, a way of escape from it.

The norm that Tillich derives from the cross, like all those
which are related only to estrangement and redemption, is a
fine tool for the exposure of man's various idolatries. But it
says nothing of the human enterprise as a response to the imperative of God the Creator. It assesses things not in their
own terms but in the light of their capacity to point toward

that from which existence is fallen. The variety and integrity of cultural ends and values tend to be swallowed up by their religious dimension. The idea of the natural provides a way to affirm that to exist means to be called by God to fulfill existence. The interaction between man and his environment has its own independent meaning and importance. God has established it; man is called to affirm it.

An interpretation of the natural faithful to Luther and Calvin would be governed by two assumptions: First, that its content cannot be specified fully without reference to Jesus Christ; second, that nonetheless it is formally implied in the Genesis account of creation. For Calvin, knowledge of God and knowledge of self are inextricably related.[11] True humanity means life oriented toward God; its proportions cannot be grasped when that relationship has been distorted. It is through the obedience of the Christ that we come to genuine knowledge of not only the nature and will of God, but also the nature and destiny of man. Revelation in Christ provides the only authentic picture of man's grandeur and misery. While Luther did not deny that the law of God is obscurely revealed in nature and more fully in the Old Testament, he insisted that men do not truly apprehend that will apart from the Christ. Able to recognize some of its demands, they seek to justify themselves by this knowledge, by their orthodoxy or piety or virtue, and so they irremediably distort even the partial truth they have grasped. If the law serves to maintain the rudiments of community, it also confirms man in his ignorance and vanity.

When Paul develops the contrast between the first and the second Adam, his meaning is that the nature of man is definitively revealed not through God's original creative activity but only through the obedience of the Son of God. What the contrast emphasizes is not the parallel between the effects of

sin and grace, the rebellious work of Adam and the reconcil-
ing work of Christ, but rather the subordination of the first
Adam to the second. The meaning of the parallel, Karl
Barth writes,

is not that the relationship between Adam and us is the expression of our true and original nature, so that we would have to
recognize in Adam the fundamental truth of anthropology to
which the subsequent relationship between Christ and us would
have to fit and adapt itself. . . . Adam is . . . the type of Him
who was to come. Man's essential and original nature is to be
found, therefore, not in Adam but in Christ. In Adam we can
only find it prefigured. Adam can therefore be interpreted only
in the light of Christ and not the other way round.[12]

Adam is only a preliminary draft, a sort of provisional definition of what manhood means. Our relationship to Jesus of
Nazareth is ontologically prior and superior to our relationship to the first Adam. It is the Christ who represents the
essential nature of man. His acceptance of the way of the
cross defines the meaning of the natural.

But though its definitive expression is Christ, the idea of
the natural is formally implied in the Genesis story. In the
confessions that comprise the Lutheran *Book of Concord,*
there is no separate article concerned with God the Creator
or with the Old Testament account of creation. There is none
because the Reformers approached the Old Testament from
the perspective of the New and read Genesis in the light of
the gospel. For Luther and Calvin, belief in a gracious Creator was not a kind of prolegomenon to full Christian commitment but the consequence of having been grasped by the
love of God in Jesus Christ. Neither reason nor nature nor
history offers any unambiguous testimony about the source of
things. The Reformers did not first affirm that God is and is
good and then go on to say that he has come among us in

Jesus of Nazareth. Because he has come among us and revealed himself in this way, we are constrained to acknowledge a gracious Creator.

From this perspective, the Genesis saga cannot be read as a scientific account of the origin of the world or as a speculative address to the question of the existence of God. Its significance does not lie in its news about the contingency of man and the magnitude of his rebellion. Nor is it primarily an affirmation of the sovereignty and absolute power of God — for that matter, the idea of *creatio ex nihilo* is nowhere explicit in Genesis at all. The story of creation and fall does not constitute an independent chapter in Biblical theology. It is a preface to the history of election that begins with the call of Abraham. The divine summons to him, this strange act through which all nations are to be blessed, illuminates everything that precedes it. The first chapters of Genesis provide a context for the covenant established with Abraham and fulfilled with Jesus of Nazareth. Both Old Testament and New are concerned with God the promise maker, whose will it is to bless everyone through his promise to Abraham. The themes of creation and covenant are inseparable. Barth calls the creation narrative the story of the establishment of the external context for the covenant, and refers to the latter as the internal basis and meaning of the work of the Creator. " The meaning of creation," he writes,

is to make possible the history of God's covenant with man which has its beginning, its centre and its culmination in Jesus Christ. The history of this covenant is as much the goal of creation as creation itself is the beginning of this history.[18]

Though rich and complete in himself, God does not will to be alone. In his sovereign freedom he determines that there should be that which is other than himself. He makes heaven and earth as a context for his covenant with creatures whose existence he does not begrudge but has himself created and preserves. He offers promises to them and finally sends his Son to be with them. He wills the life of what is not himself and does so not because it contributes to his fulfillment but in order that it might find its own fulfillment through dialogue with him. Barth cites the words of Luther that God has created the world and man through " sheer fatherly kindness and compassion, apart from any merit or worthiness of mine; for all of which I am bound to thank and praise Him, to serve Him and to be obedient, which is assuredly true." And he comments:

Do you feel in these words Luther's amazement in face of creation, of the goodness of God, in which God does not will to be alone, but to have a reality beside Himself? Creation is grace. . . . God does not grudge the existence of the reality distinct from Himself; He does not grudge it its own reality, nature and freedom. The existence of the creature alongside God is the great puzzle and miracle. . . . Is it not true that if we confront existence, not least our own existence, we can but in astonishment state the truth and reality of the fact that I *may exist,* the world may exist, although it is a reality distinct from God, although the world including man and therefore myself is not God? God . . . does not grudge existence to this other. He not only does not grudge it to him, He not only leaves it to him, He gives it to him.[14]

The theme of the first chapters of Genesis is neither divine omnipotence nor human sin. Approached from the vantage point of the gospel, creation means grace. It is the promise freely offered to Abraham and fulfilled in Christ which is the meaning and goal of creation. The distinction between God and the world and the relation between man and his environment are not the consequences of some primordial fall. They are ordained by God. They exist for the sake of the covenant.

He maintains the world in its very distinction from himself as a context for the natural life, for the kind of fulfillment that is appropriate for the creature. He is not jealous of what he has made. In a fine essay, *Christian Affirmations in a Secular Age,* Giovanni Miegge writes:

We must not allow this affirmation of the goodness, the reality and the stability of the world to be evacuated of its force by the thought of the infinite qualitative difference which exists between God and the world, time and eternity, the finite and the infinite. This difference is real. . . . But the infinite qualitative difference between the infinite and the finite is not the criterion by which the value of the finite is to be determined. Even in its infinite inferiority the finite may be good, and in fact is good; more than this, its goodness as the finite is directly related to this infinite qualitative difference which distinguishes it from God. . . . The created being is good just in so far as it is a created being, and as created being. To the reality of this goodness we must confidently hold fast.[15]

The importance of the idea of the natural lies in its witness to the true focus of the Genesis narrative, which is not on divine power but on divine love. Its function in the theology of culture is to clarify what this focus implies. What it means to be a creature cannot be stated simply in terms of divine sovereignty and human contingency or expulsion from paradise and redemption. There is another dimension. To be a creature means to be called to the employment of all the powers and liberty that God has delegated to what he has made. Man is created from the dust of the earth, but he is called to be its lord, to fill it and have dominion over it. He is called to respond to all the challenges and realize all the possibilities entailed by the life he has been given.

The context for the natural life and the call to achieve it are in no way revoked or annulled by man's estrangement.

They express the gracious will of the Creator and are not contingent upon man's faithfulness, as though it were possible for Adam's fall to contravene the intentions of his Lord. It is not the first Adam's rebellion which is primary and determinative but the covenant consummated in Christ, the covenant for whose sake God created heaven and earth. Despite man's folly and ingratitude, God preserves the realm he has created for the expanse of finite freedom and calls man to commerce with it. That commerce is tainted by man's disobedience and ambition to be like God, but it is still shaped by a divine imperative. What emerges from it still serves the fulfillment of creaturely life which is the design of the Creator — not only the ends man is compelled to seek for the sustenance of life itself, but also the rich fabric of other meanings and values woven in the course of play and other forms of cultural activity. Man has a certain inalienable freedom to pursue these things and the pressure of biological interests and the instinct for play constrain him to it.

The human enterprise reflects an intricate pattern of darkness and light. It is not entirely a realm of darkness, for even in its fallen form it remains a response to the will of its Author. The idea of the natural is an important supplement to the themes of estrangement and redemption. It bears witness to the grace of the Creator, to the positive dimensions of creatureliness, and to the divine imperative that lies at the origin of cultural activity and governs it still. It provides a standard which recognizes the integrity and importance of cultural values because it relates them to the benevolence of God.

Tillich, who represents a pervasive tendency in recent Protestant thought, equates the substance of the creation story entirely with its testimony to divine power and human finitude. This deprives it of any significance at all for the interpretation of the human enterprise. It contributes nothing that is not also expressed by the story of the Fall. The narrative of man's folly and disobedience, seen against the background of divine sovereignty, in fact provides the only perspective from which to view the human venture. The resources for the theology of culture all reside in the affirmation that man is estranged from, yet still sustained by, ultimate reality.

But this alters the focus of the Genesis story from love to power and severs the themes of creation and covenant. The creation myth is divorced from revelation in Christ, the supreme instance of deliberate divine initiative which illuminates all else. So the idea of a distinctive creaturely vocation inevitably becomes ambiguous. The meaning of creatureliness is diminished. What Genesis tells and what the idea of the natural affirms is that the Creator wills that the world should exist in its very distinction from himself, for the sake of the creatures he has made. The difficulty with Tillich, and too often with contemporary Protestantism, is not that the human venture is approached in the light of Golgotha and the expulsion from Eden, but that the proportions of the creation story are reduced until it contributes nothing at all of its own.

When human culture is interpreted only in the context of estrangement and redemption, the results are faithful neither to its reality nor to its Author. Our trouble today is not that we have too little religion but that we have too much, and it seems fated to retain its popularity until the end of the age of tranquilizers. Everyone seems to look for nostrums promising some sort of escape, and our religious evangelists are often far too willing to oblige them. But existence is a gift. It is not meant to be escaped or transcended but fulfilled. Salvation is offered in the world, not from it. We must learn to speak of the Creator again and tell that he is good.

But what is natural for man? If the idea is formally implied in Genesis, what does it mean?

BEING FOR AND BEING WITH

The first two chapters of Genesis tell of the blessing of the man whom God creates from the dust of the ground. It has four dimensions. His being in the world is established and approved by the Creator; Eden is transformed from desert to garden for his home. Man is not only affirmed in his earthliness, he is called to be lord of the earth. One aspect of this vocation is that he is invited to name every living thing — the artist's venture. To know the name of something is to have power over it. But God brings all things to Adam " and whatever the man called every living creature, that was its name " (Gen. 2:19b). Then the Lord creates Eve and calls man to be fruitful and multiply. He establishes and approves being with others. He wills man to live in community, to be with others and not by himself.

Finally, Adam and Eve are commanded to refrain from eating of the tree of the knowledge of good and evil. This is also an aspect of the blessing because God beholds them and is pleased with what he has made. He wills not only that they should live with one another, but also with him. He wants to share himself. The completion of the blessing is the commandment to refrain from the fruit of the tree. The prohibition is grace, for it means the offer of life with the Creator, being before God. Man is blessed by the call to live on the earth, with his brothers, before God. These are the dimensions of the blessing: being in the world, being over the world, being with others, being before God. The Lord, the brother, the earth — his relation to each and all of these is written into his nature.

The Lord, when he wills to create Adam, says: " 'Let us make man in our image, after our likeness. . . .' So God created man in his own image, in the image of God he created him; male and female he created them " (Gen. 1:26-27). The meaning of the reference to the image of God is obscure, but in some way it is related to the fact that man is created male and female and called to live in community. Barth has written that the " Let us " which the Creator speaks means that the image cannot be defined apart from

the differentiation and relationship, the loving co-existence and co-operation, the I and Thou, which first take place in God Himself. Is there no significance in the fact that this matter is expressed in this connexion? . . . The relationship between the summoning I in God's being and the summoned divine Thou is reflected both in the relationship of God to the man whom He has created, and also in the relationship between the I and the Thou, between male and female, in human existence itself.[16]

Man is made for life together with God and neighbor; the I can find and fulfill itself only in relation to the Thou. No matter how dubious is Barth's particular exegesis of " Let us," the nature of the blessing is captured by his identification of the *imago dei* with man's capacity to relate to God and to other selves, a capacity rooted in his ability to relate to himself and to the world in which the Lord has placed him. His divine likeness lies in his responsiveness to the calls of God and neighbor.

The image, because it is a relational affair, is not a possession but a possibility. To achieve it man must consent to the limits of creaturely life. They are an integral part of the blessing itself, for they establish communion with God. But Adam does not consent to them. He chooses what is absurd. He wants another kind of likeness. He wants to be independent, himself the arbiter of good and evil. Adam and Eve succumb to the serpent and achieve a sort of distorted and terrible likeness to God. The Creator is rich and complete in himself, Adam is not. Adam is not self-sufficient, but now he is alone. This is the bitter achievement of his ambition — loneliness. So now he must die, for death is the final confirmation and consummation of being alone.

The earth, the brother, the Lord: he turns away from God and loses his original relationship to his brother and to the world. Obedience to the Father was the condition of Adam's dominion over the earth and his freedom from domination by it. But now every aspect of the original blessing lies under a curse: Man's being in the world, by the enmity between him and the serpent. Man's being over the world, by the burden of labor. Man's being with others, by the pain of childbirth. Man's being before God, by expulsion from Eden and finally by death. It is exile from the garden that renders the curse effectual.

But when Adam is sent out from Eden, God guards him still, provides him with clothes, and allows him to live. Even though Cain is banished after the murder of Abel, he remains under divine protection. The curse on the land seems mitigated after Noah begins to cultivate the vine. After the Flood the Lord promises that " while the earth remains, seedtime and harvest, cold and heat, summer and winter, day and night, shall not cease " (Gen. 8:22). The story of Babel, which is the summary description of the demonic possibilities of human pride, is followed by the account of the election of Abraham, through whom all nations are to be blessed. And it is this act which is the conclusion and reason for the whole narrative.

When the Creator lays his curse upon Adam, the original blessing is not revoked. Blessing and curse are, together,

Adam's inheritance, and even the curse is an expression of divine concern. It means that the Creator will not abandon the estranged creature. He cherishes Adam too much to allow him to rest content in his blindness and folly. The curse is one form the blessing must assume when the blessed creature has become a sinner. But the blessing itself remains, undiminished and unaltered: " Be fruitful and multiply, and fill the earth and subdue it; and have dominion " (Gen. 1:28). The world and man's life in it are still affirmed; the call to fulfill existence and the context for its fulfillment still remain.

The involution of the original blessing and the curse, and the ambiguity of finite creativeness as both an expression of fallenness and also a response to a divine imperative, are magnificently portrayed in the juxtaposition of the tenth and eleventh chapters of Genesis. The latter is the story of Babel, the consummate stage of man's rebellion. Cultural activity is described as a deliberate attack on the sovereignty of God. The naming of things was intended to give man dominion over the earth under God. Instead, man uses his language to further his ambition to be his own god. Language is given man so he can make promises and affirm loyalties, and so imitate the nature of his covenant-swearing Author. Instead, he uses words to further his own limitless will to make a name for himself. So he is punished by the confusion of tongues. The Creator reaffirms the curse that accompanies the blessing.

But chapter ten, the table of nations, offers a very different and yet complementary account of the origin of languages. It begins:

These are the generations of the sons of Noah, Shem, Ham, and Japheth; sons were born to them after the flood. The sons of

Japheth: Gomer, Magog, Madai, Javan, Tubal, Meshech, and
Tiras. The sons of Gomer: Ashkenaz, Riphath, and Togarmah.
The sons of Javan: Elishah, Tarshish, Kittim, and Dodanim.
From these the coastland peoples spread. These are the sons of
Japheth in their lands, each with his own language, by their
families, in their nations. (Gen. 10:1-5.)

The chapter is a commentary on the original blessing of man.
It relates the diversity of human community to the commandment and opportunity to be fruitful. Though racial and linguistic differences confirm man in his isolation and estrangement, they are, first of all, signs of the graciousness of the
Creator and the consequences of his blessing. They reflect the
will of God and rebellion against his will at the same time.
Man's response to the blessing is shot through with ambiguity. It is natural and conforms to the will of God to the extent that it is shaped by the blessing itself and the nature the
Creator has given to what he has made. But it is unnatural,
too.

Yet it is the will of God that man should perfectly attain what is natural. He is always constrained to this pursuit
by a divine imperative, but it is attained only in the true humanity of Jesus of Nazareth. The image of God, never man's
possession, was always his possibility, its achievement await-
ing one who " did not count equality with God a thing to
be grasped, but emptied himself, taking the form of a servant " (Phil. 2:6b-7). This one is the completion of creation,
the concrete realization of the natural, the definitive expression of what it means to be a man.

The decisive event in the life of Jesus of Nazareth is his
acceptance of the cross. He asks his disciples, " But who do
you say that I am? " Peter answers, " You are the Christ."
Jesus responds that the vocation of the Christ is to suffer and
die, and for this he must go to Jerusalem.

And he began to teach them that the Son of man must suffer many things, and be rejected by the elders and the chief priests and the scribes, and be killed. . . . And Peter took him, and began to rebuke him. But turning and seeing his disciples, he rebuked Peter, and said, " Get behind me, Satan! For you are not on the side of God, but of men." (Mark 8:31-33.)

The prophecy is fulfilled and he is nailed to a tree. At the ninth hour, according to Mark, he utters a cry of abandonment and then, forsaken and alone, he is dead.

And when the sixth hour had come, there was darkness over the whole land until the ninth hour. And at the ninth hour Jesus cried with a loud voice, "Eloi, Eloi, lama sabachthani?" which means, "My God, my God, why hast thou forsaken me?" (Mark 15:33-34.)

There is no reason to read the cry in the context of the jubilant psalm of praise where it originally appears. At this time and in this place these are words of abandonment, not victory. The Nazarene is forsaken. He hangs there on his tree, then ventures into the darkness alone. There is no help for him, no comfort, no one to whom to turn.

The mystery of the cry of dereliction lies at the heart of the cross and the history of God's dealings with man. If there is one decisive moment in which Jesus is revealed to the eyes of faith as he who is the Christ, it is not at his baptism or transfiguration. It is not demonstrated by some miraculous exercise of power, or by a word of mercy or healing, or by a prophetic call to repentance. On the day of the crucifixion, the cry of abandonment means tragedy. But from the vantage point of Easter faith these words of anguish disclose the depths of the love of God.

It is a heroic act to die for family or friends, but Jesus does more than this. He dies expressly for those who have laughed

at him and betrayed him. Perhaps it would be greater her-
oism to die for one's enemies, if one believed that despite
their hostility their lives were worth preserving even at the
cost of one's own. But Jesus does more than this. He does not
sacrifice himself for the noble or beautiful, for the establishment. He dies expressly for the outsiders, for publicans and
outcasts, for prostitutes and thieves. He offers his life for
enemies, not friends, for the frail and corrupt, not for the
wise and strong. So Paul tells the church at Rome:

While we were yet helpless, at the right time Christ died for the
ungodly. Why, one will hardly die for a righteous man. . . . But
God shows his love for us in that while we were yet sinners Christ
died for us. (Rom: 5:6-8.)

There is nothing in the beloved which inspires this sort of
love. It is scarcely motivated by a belief in the infinite value
of the human soul. It is neither offered nor withheld in proportion to the worth of its object. It seeks out the loner, the
ugly, the vulgar. It is granted without regard for what they
believe or what they do. They are not loved because they are
valuable, they become valuable because they are loved. The
message of the cross is that whatever exists is cherished. To
be is to be loved by the crucified.

The love of the cross compels Christians to believe that
Jesus was not only a good man but one who was supremely
good. It is a heroic act to give up life for some cause or value
in which one has invested trust and loyalty. Sometimes men
must die to preserve their relation to what is good and to
keep from betraying themselves. But Jesus does something
quite different. He, the good man, lives for the sake of those
who are estranged from the good by their own lust or ignorance or frailty. And he dies for them. Because he lives *for*
them he wills to live *with* them. Not only does he teach

about the good. Not only does he bring the good, in the sense that his words and deeds exemplify it. Not only does he bring men to the good, in the sense that their wills are transformed by the power of his example. He does all this, but he also wills to participate in their own alienation from the good, in their situation of abandonment and hopelessness. He wills to stand where they stand beneath the judgment of God. And it is this mystery of love that the cry of dereliction enshrines.

He who is supremely good not only sacrifices his life for the sake of what is good, he sacrifices his own relationship to it for the sake of the lives of his lost brothers. He dies a criminal, accursed, alone. The anguish of such a death would be assuaged for one who knew himself still united with the source of life and meaning, even in the moment the light was extinguished. But Jesus does not have this solace. He is forsaken by the Father to whom he appeals. He who is blameless accepts voluntarily the destiny of those who aspire to be like God. He who is the Word and disclosure of the Father accepts the terrible reflection of divine self-sufficiency which the ambition of the creature to be like its Creator achieves, loneliness that is ratified and culminated in death. He who is one with the Father accepts the judgment to which the sinner consigns himself, isolation and abandonment. Jesus dies alone, sacrificing his own relationship to the good in order to stand in solidarity with all those who are estranged from it.

The Easter message is that he was not permitted to remain forsaken. His relation to the Father is sustained by the Father, not in spite of but because of its absolute surrender. The Easter story tells the surrender was made in freedom and love, as an act of obedience to the Father. The *kenōsis* of the Christ, his descent and self-emptying, meant standing in the place of the first Adam, torn away from the earth, friendless,

under silent skies. But this was the strait gate to his *plērosis,*
his exaltation and fulfillment, the completion of creation.
This is true Adam, strung up between a couple of thieves,
one who

> had no form or comeliness that we should look at
>   him,
> and no beauty that we should desire him.
> He was despised and rejected by men;
>   a man of sorrows, and acquainted with grief;
> and as one from whom men hide their faces
>   he was despised.
>
>   (Isa. 53:2b-3.)

Only one who is wholly in command of himself can surrender himself as Jesus does at Calvary. Only one who is
wholly in possession of himself can offer himself wholly for
others, even his own relation to the source of meaning and
value, with no strings attached. But all who are estranged
from the Creator of the self are estranged from themselves
as well. He who can surrender himself wholly possesses himself wholly, and this is to be one with the Father. In the light
of Easter, it is the cry of dereliction which testifies to the
unity of Jesus and the Creator, unity disclosed when he freely
sacrifices it in obedience to the Father, in order to stand in
the place of his fallen brothers. Because his existence is existence for others, he is the Christ, the son of the God of the
covenant, whose power is the power to be with and whose
will is the will to be for what he has made. The writer of the
letter to the Colossians calls him

the image of the invisible God, the first-born of all creation; for
in him all things were created, in heaven and on earth . . . all
things were created through him and for him. He is before all
things, and in him all things hold together. (Col. 1:15-17.)

The covenant for the sake of which creation exists is fulfilled.

Jesus is the Christ because he is the one *whose being is being for and being with, in obedience to the Father.* Being for
is an act of freedom. No kind of constraint can force a man
to will the good of another and offer him forgiveness. Being
for is an act of power. Only he who can master and possess
himself is able to give himself. Being with is an act of love.
Love is the only road to union. Being with is an act of justice. Justice maintains the integrity of those who are united,
so that being with involves genuine mutuality rather than
loss of self. Obedience to the Father means faith and loyalty,
the keeping of faith. Freedom and love, justice and loyalty,
and the power that renders them effectual — these are the ingredients of being for and being with, in obedience to the
Father.

The requirements of existence for others can never be exactly specified, for they depend upon the neighbor. Their
character is always in some measure contingent upon his
character. What are his needs? How can they be most fully
served without abrogating the other responsibilities to which
one is subject? What responsibilities have precedence and
how are they to be related to one another? Existence for others means a voyage out into terra incognita which no moral
philosopher has ever precisely mapped. The Sabbath is made
for man, not man for the Sabbath.

But existence for others, as it is disclosed in the event of the
cross, does not mean any form of being for and being with,
but one that expresses obedience to the Father. The conclusion of the parallel between Christ and Adam in the fifth
chapter of Romans is that " as by one man's disobedience
many were made sinners, so by one man's obedience many
will be made righteous " (Rom. 5:19). He who said he came

not to abolish but to fulfill the Law and the Prophets submitted himself to all the demands of the law. The theme of being for and being with cannot be divorced from that of obedience. The words and deeds of Jesus of Nazareth illustrate what such faithfulness might mean. But they are not important only or even primarily because they illustrate a way of life. Their deepest significance lies in their revelation of the nature and will of the Author of life.

The Jesus who exists for others knows that

the will of God is the will of the Creator and Governor of all nature and of all history; that there is structure and content in His will; that He is the author of the ten commandments; that He demands mercy and not sacrifice; that He requires not only obedience to Himself but love and faith in Him, and love of the neighbor whom He creates and loves. . . . His obedience is a relation to a God who is much more than an " Unconditioned," met in the moment of decision. . . . It is the obedience of a Son whose sonship is not definable as just obedience to a principle that constrains obedience.[17]

Although the content of the natural cannot and must not ever be defined in any precise way, it is clarified by this revelation of the Lord who requires man's obedience. Whatever contributes to the design of this Lord for community is the natural, no matter whether undertaken in faith or ignorance of the Christ. Whatever corrupts and erodes such life together is the unnatural. Man's vital interests constrain him to identify himself with particular and limited communities. This is natural. But he always regards these limited communities as though they were the bearers of ultimate meaning, arbiters of universal standards. That is unnatural because it precludes wider community. It is idolatrous devotion to a god who is " mine but not yours " instead of the Father who is Father of all.

Despite its extremely modest content as a standard for criticism of the human venture, the idea of the natural is important because it bears witness to the graciousness of the Creator. He maintains the world in its otherness from himself so that man might fulfill the opportunities of creaturely existence. Man is not only allowed but called to pursue the natural life and constrained to that pursuit even in the midst of his rebellion. The concept of the natural saves the theology of culture from the implicit gnosticism that is entailed by exclusive reliance on the image of the cross. It insists upon the integral relationship between the gospel and Genesis.

The idea must be recovered so that those who are disenchanted with the human venture can be called to it anew in the name of the Creator. It must be recovered so those too deeply immured in the things of this world can be called back to the Author of all things. If it provides few concrete standards itself, it prevents the absolutizing of any standards, because it is not a concatenation of principles but a mandate for life together. It involves no imperialistic norms which violate the actualities of the human enterprise. It affirms whatever implements community while judging it in the light of the Source of community. In the name of the Creator, it stresses the integrity and the importance of all the cultural ends and values that contribute to life together.

But how is all this relevant to what the artist does?

ART AND "THE NATURAL"

Because it expresses the divine imperative behind cultural activity and emphasizes the way this activity is shaped by the will of the Creator, the idea of the natural illuminates the importance of what can seem insignificant when it is viewed only in the context of man's estrangement and God's redemptive work. Play is an example. Play and the institution of the family have been the two great socializing forces in the development of the West. Some years ago Edmund Schlink, a conservative Lutheran theologian, wrote an essay on music in which, dependent on Huizinga, he defines it as a form of play. But then he tells us play is really the attempt of sinful man to escape his actual place beneath the judgment of God. Legitimate for those who have been reconciled to the Father, apart from faith in Christ it means a willful failure to recognize the damned and desperate condition of man beneath the shadow of divine wrath. Exile from Eden and the word of judgment and mercy at Calvary are the only ingredients of the perspective from which Schlink regards the arts. From this vantage point play seems a thoroughly dubious affair.[18]

But in the light of the meaning of the natural, play must be recognized as always a divine mandate — although this does not deprive it of its actual ambiguity. It is the way men learn to respect order and limits, the cement of community, even though they exclude others from their play for all kinds of wrong reasons. It shapes the competitive impulse, so that community does not degenerate into a war of all against all. It is not an evasion of the responsibilities of life but an antidote against the quest for baser pleasures that blunt compassion and sensitivity to the requirements of life together. Though we are sometimes ignorant of what our play involves, it remains something we are not only permitted but to which we are called. Schlink's inability to find any positive significance in it, apart from faith in Christ, and his failure to discriminate between forms of play more and less creative, natural and humanizing, demonstrate the impoverishment theology can suffer when the concept of the natural is jettisoned.

The idea of play has limited application to the venture of

the man of letters because it tends to obscure the way that art arises from man's elemental need to improve his acquaintance with his environment. But quite apart from its play character and its importance as our means of access to the particularity of the world, the creative act furthers the will of God because it is intrinsically an affirmation of what the natural means. Art tells of the fallenness of man and the world. All form is a humanization or correction of things that endows them with new unity and intelligibility — and so it is an implicit protest against the way the world is. Even a lyric seeks to fix and hold what in itself is too ephemeral. The emotion that art expresses can reveal man's ambivalence toward himself or others or the world he inhabits. But first of all, whatever else it may be, the creative enterprise is an avowal of the natural and a warning against everything that conspires toward the dehumanization of man.

This attempt to impose form on the confusion and flux of experience is a statement of the importance of the creative life. The existence of art is testimony to the significance of human activity, a vindication of the potentialities of the self to create and elaborate meaning. As an intelligible act of expression, art testifies to the possibility and asserts the importance of communication among men. So it is a statement of faith in the value of community. It asserts the intelligibility of human experience, its amenability to clarification and organization. It is an affirmation of the value of things finite and definite, a cherishing of the little ordinary ingredients of experience. Otherwise what reason could there be for carving up the continuum of our sensations through the use of language? It implies a foundation in the world itself for the imaginative venture, an ontic justification for what the artist does.

In the work of the man of letters, no matter how bleak the

vision he means to express, there are still involved certain
crucial assumptions about the potentialities of the self, the
importance of the creative life, the possibility and value of
communication, the intelligibility of experience and worth of
its constituents, the abiding significance of human community. So it is always an obscure witness to what is natural for
man, as well as often a protest against the failure to achieve
it. Every poem and every novel is a kind of call for community and a step toward life together, because of the way it
brings some new clarity to experience and contributes to the
redemption of language. But why must words be redeemed
and what does their redemption mean?

The dimensions of the Creator's blessing are: being in the
world, being over the world, being for and with others, being
obediently before God. Being over the world: language enables man to have dominion over the earth and escape from
domination by it. By naming things he gains power over them,
places them at the disposal of the intellect. Being with others:
language is the means by which man can make promises and
affirm loyalties. Being before God: man is not content to
live before God, he seeks to be his own god. His lust for independent mastery over the world betrays him into the
world's power. His lust for mastery over man constrains him
to warp and twist his words to deceive others. His passion to
be god compels him to warp and twist them to deceive himself. The activity of the man of letters is a sort of medicine
for this. But if he can prescribe for what ails language, no
more than anyone else does he have the prescription for what
ails man.

But language does not need to be redeemed only because
man is himself a soteriological problem. As play, as the
means by which man comes to know his world, as an indirect
witness to what is natural for man, the artist's venture must

be interpreted first of all in the context of the Genesis account of the love of God the Creator. This is also one perspective from which the redemption of language must be understood. The clarification of experience is never a task once fulfilled but an endless challenge. The world changes and the distinction between appearance and reality haunts us in ever new ways. The dynamism of history disperses the meaning of words. Precision blurs away to ambiguity. A wealth of connotation leaks away from a word and leaves only some thin and trivial denotation. Vital significance is replaced by empty formality. Revolutionary changes occur that demand some new syntax to fit the altered grammar of experience.

Scientific discoveries cause an old vision of the universe to be relegated to our folklore. Yesterday's common assumptions become anomalous today. The old shape of society is transformed in response to different challenges and the traditional vocabulary, so many of its images and metaphors, seems anachronistic. It will not capture the exigencies of the new situation. The agrarian imagery of ancient sacred texts may still stir the hearts of the inhabitants of our cities, but it has lost much of its power to persuade their minds. The gift of the man of letters to us is the rehabilitation of words, the invention of new grammars, so we can grasp the new patterns and changing meaning of our experience in some discriminating way. With every pungent image that captures the actuality of our lives, with every protest against the obfuscation of things by demagogy and sentimentality and nostalgia for what has vanished, he may succeed in the redeeming of words — challenging all the inherited preconceptions venerated more for age than truth, all the uncritical and uncriticized assumptions cherished not because they are valid but because they are familiar, all the undiscriminating and insensitive responses shaped by habit and convention more than by the situations in which we find ourselves.

In our age the health of the artist's venture seems of particular urgency and importance. Communication becomes more difficult whenever community loses its stability. Now new sociological patterns conspire time and again to render the burden of loneliness more grievous. We are no strangers to the " panurbanized " world, the asphalt jungle: the individual is estranged from the land and swallowed up in the anonymity of the city. The extent of his estrangement is evident in the remarkable belief that he is getting back to the land when he drives over it at sixty miles an hour and " looks at the view." A technological society is an extremely mobile one, and among us nomads, cultural and ethnic traditions decay, old loyalties dissolve, the unity of the family and the traditional parish system break down. And our encounters with one another grow more marginal. Technology breeds specialization; specialized men meet in ever more marginal and partial ways.

Community becomes splintered, the person is fractured. Death is the last solvent of community. Now death may well be frightening just because it has lost its mystery and abruptness and sacral quality. It becomes a familiar presence in our daily life, familiar in the constant, desolating disruptions of community which no city planner will ever obviate — present only in a minor key and diminished mode, but the more terrible because it is not the end of life but a part of life in a world bereft of its old stability. And some do not believe that even the prospect of interment at Forest Lawn is satisfactory compensation. As the postures of those who people existentialist art and literature suggest, death wears its most dreadful countenance for persons who are estranged from the traditional values of bourgeois society. So, with greater or less eloquence and restraint, the protagonist of many a novel has echoed the now familiar protest of Frederick Henry:

I was always embarrassed by the words sacred, glorious, and sacrifice and the expression in vain. We had heard them, sometimes standing in the rain almost out of earshot, so that only the shouted words came through, and had read them, on proclamations that were slapped up by billposters over other proclamations, now for a long time, and I had seen nothing sacred, and the things that were glorious had no glory and the sacrifices were like the stockyards at Chicago if nothing was done with the meat except to bury it. There were many words that you could not stand to hear and finally only the names of places had dignity. Certain numbers were the same way and certain dates and these with the names of the places were all you could say and have them mean anything. Abstract words such as glory, honor, courage or hallow were obscene beside the concrete names of villages, the numbers of roads, the names of rivers, the numbers of regiments and the dates.[19]

The recent wars, the progress of science, the present world ferment, the emergence of new kinds of community shaped by new pressures — these have had a revolutionary impact on the bourgeois tradition and the bourgeois church. And no values at all are secure from disaster in this nuclear age of the world's maturity. In Western history, men have always been assured of some kind of tenuous immortality, no matter what their religious persuasion, because of the survival of the common values in which not only themselves but their society had invested faith. But few are very sanguine about this sort of objective immortality now. The more or less cohesive vision of things we ascribe, perhaps in romantic excess, to the members of earlier societies has been splintered. Now there are many fragmentary ones which conflict and sometimes cannot be reconciled. What this means is that we

do not have a *lingua franca* in the sense in which our ances-
tors did. People with discrete visions of the world have languages that differ in subtle and inconspicuous but important
ways. So they talk at each other more than they talk with.
Stephen Dedalus, when he confronted the dean of studies at
University College, described our revisitation of Babel this
way:

The language in which we are speaking is his before it is mine.
How different are the words *home, Christ, ale, master,* on his lips
and on mine! I cannot speak or write these words without unrest
of spirit. His language, so familiar and so foreign, will always be
for me an acquired speech. I have not made nor accepted its
words. My voice holds them at bay. My soul frets in the shadow
of his language.[20]

The anatomy of a language and the way it is used reflect
and shape the values to which those who speak it are committed. A language is elaborated in such fashion that it will
sustain and advocate those values. When there is reason to
doubt their validity, or to doubt the way in which we have
been told they are related to one another, or at least to question whether they are as important and unambiguous as we
have been told, then words grow cheap. New and idiosyn-
cratic languages arise. Every profound alteration of the cultural situation involves a kind of confusion of tongues in
which there is no longer any consensus about the connotations of words. So, for a variety of reasons, our life tends to
become more fragmented, and each fragment tends to adopt
its own special language — the vocabularies of teen-agers,
of the intelligentsia, of religion, of advertising executives.
The problems of this linguistic pluralism are aggravated
by media of mass communication which foster a sort of syn-
dication of language. This is one answer to the proliferation

of tongues, but its price is high. It practices a kind of piracy for political or commercial or entertainment purposes that robs us of a language for private experience and independent judgment. The vocabulary of love is romanticized and externalized until it becomes misleading and stale. Words lose their depth. Their significance comes to lie not in what they convey but in the image they evoke: the meaning of love is dwarfed into the image of the lover.

In every imprecise phrase, every conventional response, every stereotyped emotion, every broken dialogue, there is an epiphany of death, the final disperser of community and ratifier of our isolation. Language is its accomplice, whenever the old grammar and vocabulary are not adequate to capture the exigencies of a new situation, whenever we are barred from others by our reliance on the stale commonplaces and phony sentiments that infect our speech and whose tyranny is reinforced by our laziness and indifference. In an age of revolution more vigilance than ever must be exercised on behalf of words. It is simply the dynamism of history that testifies to the validity of Allen Tate's description of the vocation of the man of letters. Language must constantly be renewed. Its redemption is one vital aspect of man's response to the divine imperative that calls him to fulfill the opportunities of existence. But the task is all the more urgent because man himself needs to be redeemed.

FALLENNESS AND THE UNNATURAL
USE OF WORDS

We use language to deceive ourselves and to dupe others. We use it to disguise our own real commitments from ourselves and to coerce commitments from others. We use it for betrayal instead of for promises. But there are two principal ways in which words are employed unnaturally. One involves the repression of experience; the other, the expression of the will to power, most notably in the instance of propaganda. In *The Principles of Art,* Collingwood writes that the root of all evil is what he calls the corruption of consciousness, because it is the source of

"fantasies," sentimentalized or bowdlerized pictures of experience, Spinoza's "inadequate ideas of affections"; and the mind that takes refuge in them from the facts of experience delivers itself into the power of the feelings it has refused to face.[21]

Men are the prey of their brute instincts and feelings until these are raised to the level of consciousness by some kind of expressive activity. When they are recognized for what they are, we can find ways to control them. But all of us tend to repress the shabbiest of our emotions and the most unpalatable dimensions of experience. So we are enslaved by what we are unwilling or unable to confront, and life loses its coherence and order. Failing to acknowledge some aspect of its inner life, the corrupt consciousness distorts and falsifies other dimensions of its experience as well because of this one dishonest omission. The uncorrupted consciousness is one that faces the feelings and desires brought within its reach. It is liberated from their tyranny because it does not shrink from the expressive activity that is necessary if they are to be defined and domesticated so that will and intellect can be the rulers of their own house. " If a given feeling is thus recognized," Collingwood writes,

it is converted from impression into idea, and thus dominated or domesticated by consciousness. If it is not recognized, it is simply . . . left unattended to, or ignored. But there is a third alternative. The recognition may take place abortively. It may be attempted, but prove a failure. . . . We direct our attention towards a certain feeling, or become conscious of it. Then we take fright at what we have recognized: not because the feeling, as an impression, is an alarming impression, but because the idea into which we are converting it proves an alarming idea. We cannot see our way to dominate it, and shrink from persevering in the attempt. We therefore give it up, and turn our attention to something less intimidating. I call this the " corruption " of consciousness; because consciousness permits itself to be bribed or corrupted in the discharge of its function. . . . It is an extremely common fact.[22]

He argues that the creative enterprise must not be defined only in terms of the novels and paintings and symphonies that emerge from it. It includes all conscious and deliberate expression of emotion. But expression is not complete apart from the embodiment of whatever it is that a man is struggling to understand. Apprehension, expression, and embodiment are inseparable. So the artist's venture fulfills our elemental need to grasp the nature of our emotions. It is vital if we are to be the masters of ourselves. It brings clarity and order to the realm of feeling and is a remedy for the corruption of consciousness.

This corruption is one cause of the unnatural use of language. We baptize aspects of experience that frighten us with the wrong names; we use words to obscure our feelings because we are ashamed of them. We find that it is much easier to rationalize than to reason. So we call lust and sentimentality by the name of love. We label as devotion to family or nation or church what is only an anguished and desperate search for any identity at all by some lost and fragmented self. We lose ourselves and forfeit the chance to become better than we are. Everything is prettified. And because we do not serve our words well, we destroy their powers to serve us.

They are blunted as we use them to slur over experience so that what scares us about it recedes from the light of consciousness. Language grows ambiguous and misleading. The use of our words to evade the realities of existence is common practice in the lives of us all. But it endangers being over the world and being with others; it is unnatural.

Men belong to a universal community, for God is the Father of all. But they depend upon particular and limited societies within this universal community, and these exercise their own legitimate claims for loyalty. To defend and preserve them, honesty must be subjected to limits. There are times when silence is more important than speech and censorship must be employed for the sake of freedom. Truth must be withheld or told only in part. But the realism that recognizes this is inseparable from the will to power that acknowledges no commitment to truth except to the truth of its own ambition. It insists that it can use words with impunity, and what it does with them threatens the survival of true community. They are warped into slogans and euphemisms and stereotypes that divide men instead of uniting them. Propaganda is meant to muddy vision rather than clarify it. It claims that some finite community is absolute, the source of universally valid standards and of infinite value. It feeds on the distinctions between men, between those who have surrendered to Moloch and those who are evil because they are different.

Perhaps no one recognized the manifold ways in which propaganda confines and confuses thought better than George Orwell. In a brief appendix to *1984*, " The Principles of Newspeak," he shows how words become a weapon in totalitarian hands. Newspeak has been devised to assure conformity and prevent any sort of ideological deviation or intellectual originality, so a heretical thought should be literally unthinkable, at least so far as thought is dependent on words. Its vocabulary was so constructed as to give exact and often very subtle expression to every meaning that a Party member could properly wish to express, while excluding all other meanings and also the possibility of arriving at them by indirect methods. . . . Newspeak was designed not to extend but to *diminish* the range of thought, and this purpose was indirectly assisted by cutting the choice of words down to a minimum. . . . Each reduction was a gain, since the smaller the area of choice, the smaller the temptation to take thought. . . . Ideas inimical to Ingsoc could only be entertained in a vague wordless form, and could only be named in very broad terms which lumped together and condemned whole groups of heresies without defining them in so doing.[23]

The populace of *1984* lives beneath slogans proclaiming that ignorance is strength. Not only is the number of words reduced; the ones that remain are stripped of their connotations. Their richness is politicized away into a single denotation. So man's capacity to grasp the texture of his experience has been that much further diminished.

In its traditional forms, play has been proscribed by the new society. It would foster a sense of fairness and a competitive spirit that could subvert the world of *1984.* So there is no art. More important, play creates a private realm, and this conflicts with the absolutist pretensions of the regime.

To do anything that suggested a taste for solitude, even to go for a walk by yourself, was always slightly dangerous. There was a word for it in Newspeak: *ownlife,* it was called, meaning individualism and eccentricity.[24]

The language of sex and love has been deliberately and thoroughly deprived of its nuances and connotations, shorn of everything but its dangerous political significance as an expression of "ownlife." After he has slept with Julia, Winston reflects:

No emotion was pure, because everything was mixed up with fear and hatred. Their embrace had been a battle, the climax a victory. It was a blow struck against the Party. It was a political act.[25]

The systematic transformation of language to serve the will to power has put to rout all possibility of authentic life together, not only for Winston and Julia but for everyone else in *1984*.

What this novel presents as future possibility is past reality and always present danger, documented by essays such as one in which George Steiner argues that "something immensely destructive" happened to the German language in the twentieth century. "Languages are living organisms," he warns,

infinitely complex, but organisms nevertheless. They have in them a certain life force, and certain powers of absorption and growth. But they can decay and they can die. A language shows that it has in it the germ of dissolution in several ways. Actions of the mind that were once spontaneous become mechanical, frozen habits (dead metaphors, stock similes, slogans). Words grow longer and more ambiguous. Instead of style there is rhetoric. Instead of precise common usage, there is jargon. Foreign roots and borrowings are no longer absorbed into the bloodstream of the native tongue. They are merely swallowed and remain an alien intrusion. All these technical failures accumulate to the essential failure: the language no longer sharpens thought but blurs it. Instead of charging every expression with the greatest available energy and directness, it loosens and disperses the intensity of feeling.[26]

Under Hitler the German language was used to convey and enforce innumerable falsehoods. Words lost their orig-

inal meaning and acquired " nightmarish definitions." The
language got " the habits of hell into its syntax." Innumerable
euphemisms were invented to disguise the truth and repress
experience, to rationalize rather than reason, and to serve racial and national versions of the will to power. Men of letters
were hunted down and silenced. Discriminating portraits of
the human condition were called decadent and supplanted
by propaganda.

As Steiner chronicles the antecedents of what happened
under National Socialism, he suggests that

When the soldiers marched off to the 1914 war, so did the words.
The surviving soldiers came back, four years later, harrowed and
beaten. In a real sense, the words did not. They remained at the
front and built between the German mind and the facts a wall
of myth. They launched the first of those big lies on which so
much of modern Germany has been nurtured: the lie of " the
stab in the back." The heroic German armies had not been de-
feated; they had been stabbed in the back by " traitors, degenerates, and Bolsheviks." [27]

Some men recognized the lies for what they were and fought
to tell the truth — the great expressionist painters, and writers such as Brecht and Rilke, Kafka and Musil, the brothers
Mann. But with the advent of Hitler the arts were regi-
mented as never before. Some men of letters were killed; others ceased to write or accepted exile. Thomas Mann chose
the latter. In an open letter to the German people, he said
that for him to remain silent would mean the betrayal of his
responsibility as an artist for the purity and renewal of the
German tongue.

Steiner tells us that the exodus of artists during these years
is of crucial importance for understanding what happened to
the language and " to the soul of which it is the voice " as
well. The health of the human enterprise depends in large

measure on the services of its men of letters. Words are volatile, susceptible to corruption and decay. We must listen to men of letters when they warn that words are ceasing to serve the ends proper to man. And it is important to remember that propaganda is not written only by totalitarian regimes. In a pluralistic and competitive society, every center of power uses language not only to express its own legitimate concerns, but also to advance the claim that its concerns are absolutely valuable. In the pronouncements of all patriotic groups, every religious establishment, each association of managers, laborers, or farmers, words are used to further a will to power that wants no restrictions at all upon its own ambitions.

The use of language to repress the actualities of experience and to implement the will to power are the primary ways in which words are used unnaturally. But they are not the only ways. The concrete meaning of existence for others depends on the needs and the nature of one's neighbor. So there is something unnatural in the ideal of frankness. What truthfulness requires cannot be fully understood in abstraction from the context in which one speaks — doctor to patient, father to son, teacher to student. On the other hand, the character of that relationship can easily be used as an excuse to avoid the demands and hazards of real dialogue.

All of us rely on linguistic conventions that have been used until they are useless, a worn little store of commonplaces, stereotypes, and slogans. Even though the pressures of daily life afford us little time to do otherwise, there is an element of the unnatural in this. It is a failure to respond to the challenges of existence — not only because we are unable but also because we are indifferent. So we live in the twilight and never at noon, for the world is lighted by our language. Our reflections on experience, the one school that prepares us to engage satisfactorily in the process of adaptation, become dull and fragmentary. We always find some way to compensate for this. The important question is what way we find.

There are always those who are eager to deny the distinction between appearance and reality and provide us with sentimental appeals to popular prejudices and piety — a flood of books, films, illustrations, magazines, and songs that bury the real contours of experience. These things do not refine feeling and illuminate existence. They confirm us in what is superficial and habitual and easy. And so comes the triumph of the marketplace mind, for conventions trap us in conventionalized experience. But the marketplace mind is never merely dull. It is always vicious, too. It uses dangerous words. The worst of them are not the profane and sacrilegious ones, not even the prettifying ones or our gutter vocabulary for sex, but little ugly words such as " nigger," " kike," " radical," " pink," " queer," " wop." They let us place an individual in a class, include him within a stereotype. So we never meet him or face the responsibilities and the joys of being together. The artist's venture is a struggle against all this. His concern is the individual and concrete, the whatness of things. His talent is to disclose through their specificity something of our shared condition. And that is the way to community. It serves the Creator's design.

EPILOGUE

Life allows us little opportunity to examine the ingredients of our experience. We ask what their import is and how they are related to one another, but what they are in themselves we have neither the time nor the patience to discover. Yet discover that we must, if we are not to have our vision of the value and relationship of things grow obscure. In one way or another, for better or worse, we satisfy the need to supplement our own grasp of the particularity of things — either by art or by surrogates for it. It is vital that we should have the arts and heed them. They are a response to the imperative of the Creator. But the artist's venture is more urgent because of man's fall, as well as tainted by it. Words need to be redeemed, and for a variety of reasons — simply because of the dynamism of history; and also because man is estranged from self, neighbor, and God. We talk *at* people instead of *with* them until we have forgotten the difference between the two. The will to power twists our words for its own purposes. We misname things because we do not want to recognize them for what they are. We rely on slogans and conventions that bar us from one another.

What the man of letters does is to fight the attrition of the meaning of words, the draining away of the connotations of things, the cleft between common usage and actuality, the reduction of heritage to convention. There is wisdom as well

as innocence in Holden Caulfield's protest against the eva-
siveness of the speech of the populace of *The Catcher in the
Rye,* and the existence of that novel is in itself a remedy for
the phoniness that finds habitation in the language of us all.

As a parable of the artist's venture, there is a memorable
scene in *Darkness at Noon.* It is the story of an old Bolshevik
named Rubashov who eventually falls from favor, is thrown
into a Moscow prison cell, and then executed. When he is
about to become a victim himself, he remembers some of
the people who were his own victims in earlier years. He had
suffered no qualms of conscience when he consigned them
to die, for he had believed the human individual could be
defined as the quotient of one million divided by one million.
But now he is no longer quite certain the value of the individual is wholly derivative from his relation to the group.
For two hundred pages Arthur Koestler prepares us for the
gesture Rubashov makes just before his death. In his anguish
and confusion he taps out the prison code for the first person
singular, 2–4.

Rubashov stopped by the wall which separated him from No.
406. The cell was empty since the departure of Rip Van Winkle.
He took off his pince-nez, looked around furtively and tapped:
2–4 . . .
He listened with a feeling of childlike shame and then knocked
again
2–4 . . .
He listened, and again repeated the same sequence of signs. The
wall remained mute. He had never yet consciously tapped the
word " I." Probably never at all. He listened.[1]

Rubashov suffers no conversion, no revelation, just a curious
toothache and a vague suspicion that something is wrong
with the assumptions by which he had lived. That is all. And
sufficient. The whole mystery of existence is contained in the

sound of a pair of glasses scratched for an instant against a wall of stone.

That is what the man of letters always does, in his own fashion. Always he is busy tapping out 2–4 against some wall of stone, refusing to let us rest content with the illusion that man is only the quotient of one million divided by one million. The artist's venture is an affirmation of the powers of the self to create meaning, and so of the meaning of human life. It is an affirmation of the possibility of significant communication, testimony to its reality, and so an avowal of the value and importance of life together. It never says I alone, but always you and I, for otherwise there would be no reason to offer one's vision to someone else. The artist's venture always says 2–4 against those who would deal too cheaply with man, and it says man was made for community. And if the existence of art affirms this much, its content affirms still more, no matter how desolating a story it tells. The artist is concerned with the specificity and whatness of the ingredients of man's experience. All his work echoes Stravinsky's words, "Let me have something finite, definite . . ." His venture calls men back from every form of revulsion in the face of what is limited and circumscribed. So the church especially has reason to heed him, for the Lord who seeks to redeem man from dehumanization is the Creator of all things.

The concern of the man of letters is neither heaven nor hell, but this earth and those who inhabit it. His concern is with the guts of things and his ambition is to bring us to some encounter with them. It is here, in the depths and not on the surfaces, we must go to school. When we follow where he leads, we find in his work intimations of judgment and grace, damnation and salvation, symbols of expiation and atonement, images of life and death, rejection and renewal. These are the perennial themes that have stuck in man's heart. But if the artist can sometimes touch the whole spectrum of religious concerns, the answers to these questions, if he knows them, it is not his vocation to give. He is not a preacher, though he serves preachers well if he leads men to the deep places where belief can be a significant act and religious themes blaze with luminosity. But his province is the province of this earth, his subject man, his vocation the redeeming of words. The word of man and not the word of God, this world and not another, these are what he is concerned to cherish and renew.

Whatever his vices as a man, if the artist does not betray his vocation to offer us some clarified vision of the subtlety of the human heart and the multifoliate texture of our experience, his work contributes to the fulfillment of the Creator's design. It is indispensable medicine for the shabbiness of common speech, the ravishing of it by the will to power, our efforts at repression, our love for cheap stereotypes, the erosion of the meaning of words by the relentless sweep of history. The God of Abraham and the Father of the Christ discloses himself as the one who is the promise maker and the promise keeper. This is what life in his image involves: being for and being with means offering promises and keeping them, swearing loyalties and not betraying them. The man of letters cannot make promise keepers of us, but he can give us language that is a fit instrument for swearing loyalties.

If the redemption of language is less than the redemption of man, and if the artist sometimes needs to be reminded of that, his service is by no means irrelevant to the greater task. The responsibility of the Christian critic is not to assess what the artist says in the light of what the church believes. Nor is it to use his work in order to discover the prevailing interpretation of man or contemporary spiritual climate. Perhaps those are things worth doing. But what is far more important is simply that the church should recognize the cruciality of what the artist does, listen to what he says, shrink from reliance upon surrogates for his venture, realize how much it serves the need of man and the will of God.

Perhaps the characteristic temper of contemporary literature, if there is one, was expressed years ago by Thomas Wolfe:

Naked and alone we came into exile. In her dark womb we did not know our mother's face; from the prison of her flesh have we come into the unspeakable and incommunicable prison of this earth. Which of us has known his brother? Which of us has looked into his father's heart? . . . Which of us is not forever a stranger and alone? [2]

If *Look Homeward, Angel* itself is not sufficient answer to the questions, it is answer enough to inspire our gratitude. From the prison of their solitude men cry out for community. The existence of every work of art affirms its value, testifies to its reality, contributes to its endurance. It attacks the barriers that separate us. It renews our commerce with the world. It rejects the world not only on account of what it lacks but also in the name of what it sometimes is. It says 2-4.

It is the wisdom of the Catholic tradition to speak of the natural and to point toward the graciousness of the Creator. Contemporary Protestantism, especially in its interpretations of cultural activity, has been damaged by its failure to do as much. But there was also wisdom in the reluctance of the Reformers to define what is natural for man apart from Jesus of Nazareth, whose being was wholly being for and being with, in obedience to the Father. He alone is the definitive expression of what it means. Because it is the Author of nature who has come among us in the Christ, we must affirm existence in this world and the divine mandate to fulfill it. That mandate lies in the Genesis story, whose focus is not on the Creator's power but on his love. Genesis tells of a God who is not jealous of what he has made, but maintains the world in its distinction from himself, so that man might attain the fulfillment appropriate for creaturely being.

Men spurn the image of God which they were created to achieve. Instead, they lust after an absurd likeness, seeking to destroy their creaturely nature and become their own gods. But the human venture is still shaped by its original divine blessing, as well as by man's rebellion. The curse accompanies the blessing but does not annul it. Despite its ambiguity, the human enterprise remains a response to which man is constrained by a divine imperative. It still achieves something of what is natural for him. Always it is called to achieve more. The artist's venture is no less ambiguous than the human venture as a whole. But it is a particularly crucial ingredient in our response to what the Creator has done.

There are always people who know no sanction against the exploitation of the earth and its citizens, others for whom the world is an object of indifference or fear, more who thirst for redemption because they want release from the burdens of creatureliness. But Christians are called to turn their eyes toward the creation into which Christ has come and which exists for the sake of the covenant, and pay its Creator the honor of calling it good. We must speak of the love of the Creator, call men to the world and affirm their venture in it in his name. We are not redeemed from the world but for it. We must talk of the natural again.

NOTES

I Theology and the Man of Letters

1. Matthew Arnold, *Essays in Criticism,* 2d series (1915 ed.), p. 2. Quoted in Basil Willey, *Nineteenth Century Studies* (Columbia University Press, 1950), p. 278.

2. Paul Tillich, *Systematic Theology* (The University of Chicago Press, 1951), Vol. I, p. 3.

3. Amos N. Wilder, *Theology and Modern Literature* (Harvard University Press, 1958).

4. T. S. Eliot, "The Waste Land," from *Collected Poems, 1909–1962* (Harcourt, Brace and World, Inc., 1963). Quotations throughout from *Collected Poems, 1909–1962* are used by permission of the publishers.

5. Rollo May, "The Significance of Symbols," *Symbolism in Religion and Literature,* ed. by Rollo May (George Braziller, 1960), pp. 22–23.

6. Wilder, *op. cit.,* p. 4.

7. Paul Tillich, *The Religious Situation,* tr. by H. Richard Niebuhr (Meridian Books, Inc., 1956), p. 38.

8. Johan Huizinga, *Homo Ludens: A Study of the Play-Element in Culture* (Beacon Press, Inc., 1955), pp. 42, 158.

9. *Ibid.,* p. 46. See also p. 173.

10. *Ibid.,* p. 8.

11. *Ibid.,* p. 8.

12. Susanne K. Langer, *Philosophical Sketches* (The Johns Hopkins Press, 1962), p. 88.

13. Eliseo Vivas, *Creation and Discovery* (Noonday Press, 1955), p. 236.

14. *Ibid.*, p. 81. See also Philip Wheelwright, *Metaphor and Reality* (Indiana University Press, 1962), especially pp. 21–44.

15. Iredell Jenkins, *Art and the Human Enterprise* (Harvard University Press, 1958), p. 123.

16. R. G. Collingwood, *The Principles of Art* (London: Oxford University Press, 1938), pp. 303–304. See Jenkins, *op. cit.*, p. 104.

17. Vivas, *op. cit.*, p. 95.

18. Collingwood, *op. cit.*, pp. 308–309.

19. Langer, *Philosophical Sketches,* pp. 90–91. See also Susanne K. Langer, *Feeling and Form* (Charles Scribner's Sons, 1953), pp. 31–32.

20. Owen Barfield, *Poetic Diction: A Study in Meaning* (London: Faber & Faber, Ltd., 1928), p. 143.

21. Jenkins, *op. cit.*, p. 4.

22. *Ibid.*, p. 116.

23. *Ibid.*, pp. 76–77.

24. Vivas, *op. cit.*, pp. 140–141. See also pp. 137–138.

25. T. S. Eliot, "Burnt Norton," *op. cit.*

26. T. S. Eliot, "Choruses from 'The Rock,'" *op. cit.*

27. Allen Tate, *The Man of Letters in the Modern World* (Meridian Books, Inc., 1955), p. 22.

28. Eugène Ionesco, *The Bald Soprano,* from *Four Plays,* tr. by Donald M. Allen, p. 39. Copyright © 1958, by Grove Press, Inc. Used by permission of the publishers.

II Paul Tillich and the Message of the Cross

1. Paul Tillich, *The Protestant Era,* tr. by James Luther Adams (The University of Chicago Press, 1948), pp. xv–xvi.

2. Paul Tillich, "Über die Idee einer Theologie der Kultur," *Religionsphilosophie der Kultur* (Berlin: Reuther und Reichard, 1919). I am indebted to Prof. William B. Green, of Vassar College, for a translation of this essay (mimeographed and privately circulated, 1961).

3. Tillich, *The Protestant Era*, p. xv. See also Paul Tillich, *Theology of Culture*, ed. by Robert C. Kimball (London: Oxford University Press, 1959), pp. 5–8.

4. Paul Tillich, *Dynamics of Faith* (Harper & Brothers, 1957), pp. 45–46.

5. Paul Tillich, *The Interpretation of History*, tr. by N. A. Rasetzki and Elsa Talmey (Charles Scribner's Sons, 1936), p. 50.

6. Tillich, *Theology of Culture*, p. 22. See also Paul Tillich, "Authority and Revelation," *The Official Register of Harvard University*, Vol. XLIX, No. 8 (April 7, 1952), p. 27: "Man is never left alone without the revealing presence of the ground of his being and meaning."

7. James Luther Adams, "Tillich's Concept of the Protestant Era," *The Protestant Era*, p. 299.

8. Tillich, *Theology of Culture*, pp. 12–15, 24–26.

9. Paul Tillich, "Theology and Symbolism," *Religious Symbolism*, ed. by F. Ernest Johnson (Institute for Religious and Social Studies, 1955), pp. 107–116.

10. Paul Tillich, "The Problem of Theological Method," *Journal of Religion*, Vol. XXVII (Jan., 1947), pp. 16–26.

11. Tillich, *The Protestant Era*, pp. xi–xii.

12. *Ibid.*, p. xiv.

13. *Ibid*, p. 163.

14. Tillich, *The Interpretation of History*, p. 223.

15. *Ibid.*, pp. 222–223.

16. Tillich, *Systematic Theology*, II, p. 6.

17. The theory of knowledge ecstatic naturalism implies is "belief-ful realism," which looks toward the inner creative infinity of Being, not some transcendent spiritual realm. It does not extrapolate from the ontological awareness of ultimate reality "a world behind the world." See Tillich, *The Protestant Era*, p. 82.

18. Tillich, *Systematic Theology*, II, p. 7.

19. *Ibid.*, p. 8.

20. Tillich, *The Protestant Era*, p. 163.

21. Tillich, "Über die Idee einer Theologie der Kultur."

22. Tillich, *The Protestant Era*, pp. 217–218.

23. Tillich, *Systematic Theology,* I, p. 131.

24. *Ibid.,* pp. 239–240.

25. Tillich, *Dynamics of Faith,* pp. 96–97.

26. Tillich, *Theology of Culture,* p. 60.

27. *Ibid.,* p. 66.

28. Paul Tillich, " Existential Analyses and Religious Symbols," *Contemporary Problems in Religion,* ed. by Harold A. Basilius (Wayne State University Press, 1956), pp. 35–55.

29. Tillich, *Dynamics of Faith,* p. 42.

30. Ben F. Kimpel, *Religious Faith, Language, and Knowledge,* p. 72. Quoted in Gustave Weigel, " Myth, Symbol and Analogy," *Religion and Culture, Essays in Honor of Paul Tillich,* ed. by Walter Leibrecht (Harper & Brothers, 1959), p. 126.

31. Tillich, *Dynamics of Faith,* pp. 97–98.

32. Tillich, *Systematic Theology,* II, p. 123.

33. Tillich, *Theology of Culture,* p. 67.

34. Tillich, *Systematic Theology,* I, p. 133.

35. *Ibid.,* p. 134.

36. *Ibid.,* p. 134.

37. And, according to Tillich, theology gains the freedom it must have from the changing conclusions of historical research.

38. For a brilliant critique, see Robert E. Cushman, " The Christology of Paul Tillich," *The Heritage of Christian Thought, Essays in Honor of Robert Lowry Calhoun,* ed. by Robert E. Cushman and Egil Grislis (Harper & Row, Publishers, Inc., 1965), pp. 166–181.

39. George H. Tavard, *Paul Tillich and the Christian Message* Charles Scribner's Sons, 1962), p. 80.

40. Tillich, *Systematic Theology,* I, p. 252.

41. Tillich, *The Protestant Era,* p. 217.

42. Tillich, *Systematic Theology,* I, pp. 253–254.

43. *Ibid.,* p. 252.

44. Tillich, *Systematic Theology,* II, p. 8. See also Paul Tillich, *Biblical Religion and the Search for Ultimate Reality* (The University of Chicago Press, 1955), pp. 74–75.

45. Tillich, *Systematic Theology,* I, p. 248.

46. Tillich, *The Interpretation of History*, p. 271.

47. Tillich, *Systematic Theology*, I, pp. 255–256.

48. Tillich, *Systematic Theology*, II, p. 44.

49. Paul Tillich, *Love, Power and Justice* (Oxford University Press, 1954), p. 110.

50. Tillich, *Systematic Theology*, II, p. 40.

51. See Reinhold Niebuhr, "Biblical Thought and Ontological Speculation in Tillich's Theology," *The Theology of Paul Tillich*, ed. by Charles W. Kegley and Robert W. Bretall (The Macmillan Company, 1952), pp. 216–227.

52. Tillich, *Systematic Theology*, II, p. 40.

53. Tillich, *The Protestant Era*, p. 57.

54. Tillich, "Über die Idee einer Theologie der Kultur." See also *Systematic Theology*, I, pp. 15–16.

55. Tillich, "Über die Idee einer Theologie der Kultur."

56. Tillich, *The Protestant Era*, p. 46.

57. Tillich, *The Religious Situation*, p. 40.

58. See James Luther Adams, *op. cit.*, p. 298.

59. Tillich, *Systematic Theology*, I, p. 40. See also Paul Tillich and T. M. Greene, "Authentic Religious Art," *Masterpieces of Religious Art* (Art Institute of Chicago, 1954).

60. Paul Tillich, "Existentialist Aspects of Modern Art," *Christianity and the Existentialists*, ed. by Carl Michalson (Charles Scribner's Sons, 1956), pp. 133–134.

61. Tillich, *Systematic Theology*, I, p. 40.

62. Tillich, "Über die Idee einer Theologie der Kultur."

63. Tillich, *Theology of Culture*, p. 72.

64. Paul Tillich, "Art and Ultimate Reality," *Art and the Craftsman*, ed. by Joseph Harned and Neil Goodwin (Southern Illinois University Press, 1961), pp. 185–200.

65. *Ibid.*, p. 189.

66. *Ibid.*, p. 192.

67. *Ibid.*, p. 194.

68. *Ibid.*, p. 195.

69. Tillich, *Theology of Culture*, p. 73.

70. *Ibid.*, p. 74. See "Art and Ultimate Reality," pp. 196, 199.

71. Tillich, *Theology of Culture,* p. 75.

72. Tillich, "Existentialist Aspects of Modern Art," p. 138.

73. *Ibid.,* p. 137.

74. Tillich, *Theology of Culture,* p. 178.

75. Tillich, "Existentialist Aspects of Modern Art," p. 144.

76. Paul Tillich, "Theology and Architecture," *Architectural Forum,* Vol. CIII, No. 6 (Dec., 1955), p. 132.

77. Paul Tillich, "The World Situation," *The Christian Answer,* ed. by Henry P. Van Dusen (Charles Scribner's Sons, 1945), p. 10.

78. *Ibid.,* p. 10.

79. *Ibid.,* p. 11.

80. *Ibid.,* p. 29.

81. *Ibid.,* p. 30: "Only those aesthetic works showed creativity and progress which either were in harmony with the general trend toward a mechanized naturalism or anticipated revolutionary opposition to it."

82. *Ibid.,* p. 30. For a similar analysis, see Paul Tillich, *The Courage to Be* (Yale University Press, 1952), pp. 137–143.

83. Tillich, "Art and Ultimate Reality," pp. 186–187.

84. Tillich, "The World Situation," p. 9.

85. See John Canaday, *Mainstreams of Modern Art* (Henry Holt & Co., Inc., 1959), p. 340: "As a point of departure for any explanation of his art, two of Cézanne's own comments are more helpful than any others. . . . 'I want to do Poussin over again, after nature,' and 'I want to make of impressionism something solid and durable like the art of the museums.'"

86. Jacques Maritain, *Creative Intuition in Art and Poetry* (Meridian Books, Inc., 1955), p. 299. This is the first volume of the A. W. Mellon Lectures in the Fine Arts. Copyright 1953 by the Trustees of the National Gallery of Art, Washington, D.C., and published for Bollingen Foundation, Inc., by Pantheon Books, Inc. Quotations throughout are used by permission of the Bollingen Foundation and The Harvill Press, Ltd.

87. Tillich, *The Protestant Era,* p. 59.

III   Nicolas Berdyaev and the Image of Consummation

1. Nicolas Berdyaev, *Solitude and Society,* tr. by George Reavey (London: Geoffrey Bles, Ltd., 1938), p. 24.

2. Nicolas Berdyaev, *The Beginning and the End,* tr. by R. M. French (London: Geoffrey Bles, Ltd., 1952), p. 154.

3. Nicolas Berdyaev, *Truth and Revelation,* tr. by R. M. French (Harper & Brothers, 1953), p. 68.

4. Nicolas Berdyaev, *Slavery and Freedom,* tr. by R. M. French (Charles Scribner's Sons, 1944), pp. 29–30.

5. *Ibid.,* pp. 130–131.

6. Nicolas Berdyaev, *Dream and Reality,* tr. by Katherine Lampert (The Macmillan Company, 1951), pp. 97–98, 286. See also Nicolas Berdyaev, *The Destiny of Man,* tr. by Natalie Duddington (Charles Scribner's Sons, 1937), pp. 2–9; and *Solitude and Society,* pp. 48 ff.

7. Nicolas Berdyaev, *Spirit and Reality,* tr. by George Reavey (Charles Scribner's Sons, 1939), pp. 52–53. See also *Dream and Reality,* p. 29.

8. Berdyaev, *Solitude and Society,* p. 62. But he rejects ontological dualism as an error of the objectified consciousness; the concept of Being is a transcendental illusion. See Nicolas Berdyaev, *The Meaning of the Creative Act,* tr. by D. Lowrie (London: Victor Gollancz, Ltd., 1955), pp. 15–16.

9. Berdyaev, *The Beginning and the End,* pp. 105–107.

10. Berdyaev, *Spirit and Reality,* pp. 114–115.

11. Berdyaev, *The Destiny of Man,* p. 29.

12. *Ibid.,* pp. 24–26.

13. Nicolas Berdyaev, *Dostoevski,* tr. by Donald Attwater (Meridian Books, Inc., 1957), p. 85. See *Dream and Reality,* p. 178.

14. Berdyaev, *The Meaning of the Creative Act,* pp. 136–137. See *Truth and Revelation,* pp. 55–56.

15. Berdyaev, *Truth and Revelation,* pp. 52–53.

16. Berdyaev, *Dream and Reality,* p. 179.

17. Berdyaev, *Truth and Revelation,* p. 112.

18. Nicolas Berdyaev, *The Realm of Spirit and the Realm of*

Caesar, tr. by D. Lowrie (London: Victor Gollancz, Ltd., 1952), p. 39. See *Truth and Revelation,* p. 56; also Matthew Spinka, "Nicolas Berdyaev," *Christianity and the Existentialists,* p. 68.

19. Berdyaev, *Dream and Reality,* p. 1.

20. *Ibid.,* p. 83. See *Slavery and Freedom,* p. 12.

21. Berdyaev, *Dream and Reality,* pp. 57–58.

22. *Ibid.,* p. 58. See Nicolas Berdyaev, *Freedom and the Spirit,* tr. by Oliver F. Clarke (London: Geoffrey Bles, Ltd., 1935), p. 18.

23. Berdyaev, *Dream and Reality,* p. 57.

24. *Ibid.,* p. 175.

25. Berdyaev, *Truth and Revelation,* pp. 56, 118.

26. Berdyaev, *Dream and Reality,* pp. 174–175. See *Freedom and the Spirit,* p. 176.

27. Berdyaev, *The Meaning of the Creative Act,* p. 151.

28. Berdyaev, *Dostoevski,* pp. 70–82. See also *The Realm of Spirit and the Realm of Caesar,* pp. 104–105.

29. Berdyaev, *Freedom and the Spirit,* pp. 126–127.

30. Berdyaev, *The Meaning of the Creative Act,* p. 96. Also *Dream and Reality,* pp. 207–208.

31. Berdyaev, *Freedom and the Spirit,* pp. 214–221.

32. Berdyaev, *The Meaning of the Creative Act,* pp. 78–81. Also Nicolas Berdyaev, *The Russian Idea,* tr. by R. M. French (The Macmillan Company, 1948), pp. 172–174; *Slavery and Freedom,* pp. 44–45.

33. Berdyaev, *Truth and Revelation,* p. 50.

34. Berdyaev, *Freedom and the Spirit,* pp. 209–210.

35. *Ibid.,* p. 22. See *Slavery and Freedom,* pp. 71, 259–261.

36. See Berdyaev, *Dream and Reality,* p. 300. The historical revelation is "exoteric," subordinate to an intuitive, mystical apprehension of divine love.

37. Berdyaev, *The Destiny of Man,* pp. 32–33. Also pp. 27 ff., 53–54.

38. Berdyaev, *The Beginning and the End,* p. 188. See pp. 183 ff., and also *The Destiny of Man,* pp. 128–129.

39. Collingwood, *op. cit.,* p. 304.

40. Berdyaev, *The Meaning of the Creative Act,* pp. 323–324. Also Nicolas Berdyaev, *The End of Our Time,* tr. by Donald Attwater (Sheed & Ward, Ltd., 1933), pp. 106–108; *The Beginning and the End,* pp. 173–179.

41. Berdyaev, *Slavery and Freedom,* pp. 127–128.

42. Berdyaev, *Dream and Reality,* p. 214.

43. Berdyaev, *The Beginning and the End,* p. 188.

44. Berdyaev, *Spirit and Reality,* p. 59.

45. Berdyaev, *The Beginning and the End,* pp. 190–192.

46. They are not so much chronological stages as different orientations of the spirit. See Nicolas Berdyaev, *The Meaning of History,* tr. by George Reavey (Meridian Books, Inc., 1962), *passim.*

47. *Ibid.,* pp. 180 ff.

48. Berdyaev, *Slavery and Freedom,* pp. 117–130.

49. Berdyaev, *The Meaning of the Creative Act,* pp. 137–138, 247–249.

50. Berdyaev offers no Biblical support for what he says of creativity. If it were a response to a divine command, creativity would be mere obedience. See Berdyaev, *The Meaning of the Creative Act,* pp. 96–99.

51. *Ibid.,* p. 225.

52. Berdyaev, *Slavery and Freedom,* p. 241. Also Nicolas Berdyaev, *The Divine and the Human,* tr. by R. M. French (London: Geoffrey Bles, Ltd., 1949), p. 139.

53. Berdyaev, *The Meaning of the Creative Act,* p. 225.

54. Berdyaev, *Freedom and the Spirit,* p. 18.

55. *Ibid.,* pp. 52–61.

56. *Ibid.,* pp. 52–53.

57. Berdyaev, *Dream and Reality,* pp. 45–46. See *Dostoevski,* p. 25.

58. Berdyaev, *The Meaning of the Creative Act,* pp. 227–229.

59. Berdyaev, *The Meaning of History,* p. 123.

60. Berdyaev, *The Meaning of the Creative Act,* pp. 237–247.

61. Berdyaev, *Dream and Reality,* p. 175.

62. Igor Stravinsky, *Poetics of Music in the Form of Six Lessons,*

tr. by Arthur Knodel and Ingolf Dahl (Vintage Books, Inc., 1959), pp. 66–68.

63. *Ibid.,* p. 79.

64. *Ibid.,* p. 79.

65. *Ibid.,* pp. 68–69.

66. W. B. Yeats, " For Anne Gregory," from *Collected Poems of W. B. Yeats* (The Macmillan Company, 1956).

67. Yeats, " A Prayer for Old Age," *op. cit.*

IV　Art as Response to the Creator

1. Jacques Maritain, *Art and Scholasticism,* tr. by J. F. Scanlan (London: Sheed & Ward, Ltd., 1939), p. 80.

2. Jacques Maritain, *The Range of Reason* (Charles Scribner's Sons, 1952), p. 25.

3. Denis de Rougemont, "Religion and the Mission of the Artist," *Spiritual Problems in Contemporary Literature,* ed. by Stanley Romaine Hopper (Harper & Brothers, 1957), p. 186.

4. The A. W. Mellon Lectures in the Fine Arts for 1952, National Gallery of Art, Washington, D.C.

5. Maritain, *Creative Intuition,* p. 3.

6. *Ibid.,* p. 3.

7. *Ibid.,* pp. 16–17.

8. *Ibid.,* p. 29.

9. *Ibid.,* p. 26.

10. *Ibid.,* p. 28.

11. *Ibid.,* p. 5.

12. Maritain, *The Range of Reason,* p. 12.

13. *Ibid.,* p. 14.

14. Maritain, *Creative Intuition,* p. 8. See also p. 210. On the idea of intentionality, see Jacques Maritain, *The Degrees of Knowledge,* tr. by Bernard Wall and M. B. Adamson (Charles Scribner's Sons, 1939), pp. 134–143.

15. Maritain, *Creative Intuition,* p. 83.

16. *Ibid.,* p. 85.

17. Maritain, *The Range of Reason,* p. 18.

18. Maritain, *Creative Intuition,* p. 91.

19. *Ibid.,* p. 91.

20. *Ibid.,* pp. 159–160.

21. *Ibid.,* pp. 128–135.

22. *Ibid.,* p. 317.

23. *Ibid.,* p. 210.

24. *Ibid.,* p. 85.

25. *Ibid.,* p. 269.

26. *Inter alia,* II Cor. 4:4; Gal. 4:3, 9; Eph. 1:21, 6:12.

27. Jacques Maritain, *The Responsibility of the Artist* (Charles Scribner's Sons, 1960), p. 29.

28. *Ibid.,* pp. 39–41.

29. *Ibid.,* p. 73.

30. From *Christ and Apollo,* by William F. Lynch, S.J., p. 15. © Sheed and Ward, Inc., 1960. Quotations throughout used by permission of the publishers.

31. *Ibid.,* p. xiv.

32. *Ibid.,* p. 13.

33. *Ibid.,* p. 15.

34. *Ibid.,* p. 12.

35. *Ibid.,* p. 8.

36. *Ibid.,* p. 113.

37. *Ibid.,* p. 113.

38. *Ibid.,* p. 129.

39. *Ibid.,* p. 141.

40. *Ibid.,* p. 146.

41. From James Joyce, *A Portrait of the Artist as a Young Man,* p. 260. Copyright 1916 by B. W. Huebsch, Inc., and 1944 by Nora Joyce. Quotations throughout are reprinted by permission of The Viking Press, Inc.

42. *Ibid.,* p. 197.

43. *Ibid.,* p. 255.

44. See Allen Tate, "The Symbolic Imagination," "The Angelic Imagination," and "Our Cousin, Mr. Poe," *The Man of Letters in the Modern World,* pp. 93–145.

45. Lynch, *op. cit.,* p. xiv.

46. *Ibid.,* p. 187.
47. *Ibid.,* p. 189.
48. *Ibid.,* p. 192.
49. *Ibid.,* pp. 192–193.
50. *Ibid.,* p. xiii.
51. Étienne Gilson, *Painting and Reality* (Pantheon Books, 1957), p. 60. These are the A. W. Mellon Lectures in the Fine Arts for 1955. Copyright 1957 by the Trustees of the National Gallery of Art, Washington, D.C., and published for Bollingen Foundation, Inc., by Pantheon Books, Inc. Quotations throughout are used by permission of the Bollingen Foundation and Routledge & Kegan Paul, Ltd.
52. *Ibid.,* p. 33.
53. *Ibid.,* p. 187.
54. *Ibid.,* p. 137.
55. *Ibid.,* p. 286.
56. *Ibid.,* p. 269.
57. *Ibid.,* p. 130.
58. *Ibid.,* p. 154.
59. *Ibid.,* p. 59.
60. *Ibid.,* p. 59.
61. *Ibid.,* pp. 242 ff.
62. *Ibid.,* p. 63.
63. *Ibid.,* p. 204.
64. *Ibid.,* p. 182.
65. *Ibid.,* p. 184.
66. *Ibid.,* p. 299.
67. *Ibid.,* pp. 126–127.
68. *Ibid.,* p. 127.
69. *Ibid.,* p. 136.
70. *Ibid.,* p. 289.
71. *Ibid.,* p. 288.
72. *Ibid.,* p. 288.
73. *Ibid.,* p. 121.
74. *Ibid.,* p. 285.
75. *Ibid.,* p. 294.

76. *Ibid.,* p. 295.

77. *Ibid.,* p. 209.

78. Louis Arnaud Reid, *A Study in Aesthetics* (The Macmillan Company, 1931), p. 321.

79. Joseph Albers, " Art and the Artist," *Art and the Craftsman,* p. 275.

80. Albert Camus, *The Rebel,* tr. by Anthony Bower (Vintage Books, Inc., 1960), p. 256.

V Art and the Natural

1. Camus, *The Rebel,* p. 253.

2. Albert Camus, *The Plague,* tr. by Stuart Gilbert (Alfred A. Knopf, Inc., 1948), p. 232.

3. Thomas Mann, *Dr. Faustus,* tr. by H. T. Lowe-Porter (Alfred A. Knopf, Inc., 1948), p. 497. Used by permission of the publisher.

4. Gilson, *op. cit.,* p. 127.

5. Stravinsky, *op. cit.,* p. 66.

6. Vivas, *op. cit.,* p. 89.

7. H. Richard Niebuhr, *Christ and Culture* (Harper & Brothers, 1951), p. 143.

8. Jacques Maritain, *Man and the State* (The University of Chicago Press, 1951), p. 90.

9. *Ibid.,* p. 90.

10. Dietrich Bonhoeffer, *Ethics,* ed. by Eberhard Bethge (The Macmillan Company, 1955), p. 101.

11. See, for example, T. F. Torrance, *Calvin's Doctrine of Man* (London: Lutterworth Press, 1949); Karl Barth, *The Knowledge of God and the Service of God According to the Teaching of the Reformation,* tr. by J. L. M. Haire and Ian Henderson (London: Hodder & Stoughton, Ltd., 1938); Edmund Schlink, *Theology of the Lutheran Confessions,* tr. by Paul F. Koehneke and H. J. A. Bouman (Muhlenberg Press, 1961).

12. Karl Barth, *Christ and Adam,* tr. by T. A. Smail (Edinburgh: Oliver and Boyd, Ltd., 1956), p. 6.

13. Karl Barth, *Church Dogmatics,* Vol. III, Part 1, ed. by G. W. Bromiley and T. F. Torrance (Edinburgh: T. & T. Clark, 1958), p. 42.

14. Karl Barth, *Dogmatics in Outline,* tr. by G. T. Thomson (London: SCM Press, Ltd., 1949), p. 54.

15. Giovanni Miegge, *Christian Affirmations in a Secular Age,* tr. by Stephen Neill (Oxford University Press, 1958), pp. 116–117.

16. Barth, *Church Dogmatics,* Vol. III, Part 1, p. 196.

17. H. Richard Niebuhr, *op. cit.,* pp. 24–25.

18. Edmund Schlink, *Zum theologischen Problem der Musik* (Tübingen: J. C. B. Mohr (Paul Siebeck), 1950).

19. Ernest Hemingway, *A Farewell to Arms* (Modern Standard Authors Edition, Charles Scribner's Sons, 1953), p. 191. Used by permission of the publishers.

20. Joyce, *op. cit.,* p. 221.

21. Collingwood, *op. cit.,* p. 224.

22. *Ibid.,* p. 217. See also p. 284.

23. George Orwell, *1984* (Harcourt, Brace and World, Inc., 1949), pp. 303 ff. Used by permission of the publisher.

24. *Ibid.,* pp. 81–82.

25. *Ibid.,* p. 128.

26. George Steiner, " The Hollow Miracle — Notes on the German Language," *The Reporter,* Vol. XXII, No. 4 (Feb. 18, 1960), p. 36. Copyright 1960 by The Reporter Magazine Company. Used by permission of the author and publisher.

27. *Ibid.,* p. 37.

Epilogue

1. Arthur Koestler, *Darkness at Noon,* tr. by Daphne Hardy (Random House, Inc., 1941), p. 254.

2. Thomas Wolfe, *Look Homeward, Angel* (Charles Scribner's Sons, 1929), epigraph. Used by permission of the publisher.